Achieving Results

Four Stages to Off-the-Chart Excellence

Lorna Riley, CSP

A Crisp Fifty-Minute™ Series Book

This Fifty-Minute™ book is designed to be "read with a pencil." It is an excellent workbook for self-study as well as classroom learning. All material is copyright-protected and cannot be duplicated without permission from the publisher. *Therefore, be sure to order a copy for every training participant by contacting:*

THOMSON

NETg

1-800-442-7477 • 25 Thomson Place, Boston MA • www.courseilt.com

Achieving Results

Four Stages to Off-the-Chart Excellence

Lorna Riley, CSP
Certified Speaking Professional

CREDITS:

Product Manager: **Debbie Woodbury**
Production Editor: **Genevieve McDermott**
Editor: **Luann Rouff**
Production Artists: **Nicole Phillips, Rich Lehl, and Betty Hopkins**
Manufacturing: **Stephanie Porreca**
Cartoonist: **Ralph Mapson**

For more information contact:

NETg
25 Thomson Place
Boston, MA 02210

Or find us on the Web at **www.courseilt.com**

For permission to use material from this text or product, submit a request online at www.thomsonrights.com.

Trademarks
Crisp Fifty-Minute Series is a trademark of NETg. Some of the product names and company names used in this book have been used for identification purposes only, and may be trademarks or registered trademarks of their respective manufacturers and sellers.

Disclaimer
NETg reserves the right to revise this publication and make changes from time to time in its content without notice.

ISBN 1-56052-609-2
Library of Congress Catalog Card Number 2001089534
Printed in the United States

2 3 4 5 GP 08 07 06

Learning Objectives For:

ACHIEVING RESULTS

The objectives for *Achieving Results* are listed below. They have been developed to guide the user to the core issues covered in this book.

THE OBJECTIVES OF THIS BOOK ARE TO HELP THE USER:

1) Gain an overview of a four-stage process for consistently achieving desired results

2) Explore 14 practical applications for using the four-stage process for personal and professional results

3) Learn how to define worthwhile results

4) Understand the essential tasks and guidelines for each stage

ASSESSING PROGRESS

NETg has developed a Crisp Series **assessment** that covers the fundamental information presented in this book. A 25-item, multiple-choice and true/false questionnaire allows the reader to evaluate his or her comprehension of the subject matter. To download the assessment and answer key, go to www.courseilt.com and search on the book title, or call 1-800-442-7477.

Assessments should not be used in any employee selection process.

About the Author

Lorna Riley, certified speaking professional, is the founder and president of the American Training Association. As a professional speaker, trainer, consultant, author, and facilitator, she has inspired results both here and abroad in areas such as banking, retail, automotive, health care, associations, technology, information services, hospitality, travel, real estate, insurance, and other product- and service-driven organizations.

Lorna's career encompasses a wide range of experience, including sales executive, sales trainer, business owner, classical pianist, teacher, computer graphic artist, marketing director, and banking officer. This diversity has given her a unique perspective on the common denominators for success and helped increase her personal productivity and sales by over 600%.

Lorna frequently contributes to trade publications and shares her unique philosophy of success in internationally known seminars, workshops, keynote presentations, and interviews with radio and television audiences.

Lorna is a member of the National Speakers Association and the author of *Quest for Your Best: A Roadmap for Finding Fulfillment in a Challenging World*, *76 Ways to Build a Straight Referral Business ASAP!*, *The Movie Lover's Cookbook: Reel Meals*, and *Acts of Love*. She has also written and produced several audiocassettes, including *The Power Pak: The Three Most Powerful Skills for Creating Success*, *Proactive Time Management*, and *Memory Management*.

Readers can contact Lorna Riley at the following:

Lorna Riley
American Training Association
2455 Flametree Lane
Vista, CA 92084
tel 760-639-4020   fax 760-639-4023
Email: lorna@lornariley.com   www.lornariley.com

Preface

The inspiration for *Achieving Results* came from the work of Dr. Joseph Campbell, a scholar known for his study of comparative mythology. Campbell found that many myths, particularly those about heroes, follow a similar process. There is a departure from the familiar, help along the way, challenges to be faced, and outcomes to the journey.

The sequence of stages in these age-old myths reveals a road map that can be used today to achieve desired results, especially in times of chaos and change. The more we prepare for the challenges ahead, the more control we have over the outcomes. To make this roadmap applicable to our modern lives, I modified the language for my seminars. It quickly proved to be an effective methodology for not only achieving desired results, but off-the-chart results—those achievements that not only meet but exceed our expectations.

Following is the four-stage process:

Stage 1 HOME: Deciding what you want

Stage 2 HELP: Getting help and creating an action plan

Stage 3 CHALLENGE: Testing the plan

Stage 4 PRIZE: Reaping the results

Achieving Results represents over 60 years of comparative study regarding the common denominators of success. Some say we travel many roads. I believe there is one road, traveled in an infinite number of ways. Let us begin.

Lorna Riley

Lorna Riley

Contents

Stage 3: Challenge–Testing the Plan

Stage 4: Prize–Reaping the Results

Summary: Putting the Process to Work

Achieving Desired Results

> " *The most painful distance in the world is between where you are and where you want to be.*"
>
> —Lorna Riley

2

Knowing What You Want

Deep within many of us is a search for a way—a way to be, a way to thrive, a way out, a way to have. If you are one of these seekers, the good news is that achieving the results you want can be learned.

Everything we do produces a result, so results matter. The first part of the challenge is knowing what you want. What is it for you? Winning the lottery? Total health? Bigger profits? Meaningful relationships? You can't know your way until you know what you want. Take a few minutes to define your *desired results*:

What result would you like to achieve as a result of reading this book?

_____

_____

Your desired results may fall into one or more of the following categories. Check (✔) all those that apply:

❏ Personal development   ❏ Risk taking

❏ Professional development   ❏ Project management

❏ Leadership development   ❏ Spiritual evolution

❏ Change management   ❏ Heroic transformation

❏ Problem solving   ❏ Scientific methodology

❏ Flow: the optimal experience* ❏ Training cycle

❏ Team building   ❏ Continuous learning

All of the preceding categories of results have one thing in common: *process!*

They all achieve results in the same way. Becoming a leader, managing change, managing a project, solving a problem, and continuous learning can all be achieved by going through the same four stages that you are about to learn.

What's the benefit to you? Suppose that you want to solve a problem. If you follow the four-stage process, not only will you solve the problem, you'll also manage a risk, manage change, manage a project, develop leadership skills, find continuous learning, and grow personally, professionally, and spiritually—all at the same time.

---

*Flow is the word people use to describe their state of mind when it is "harmoniously ordered." Sports, hobbies, games, and certain tasks produce a suspended, pleasurable state, causing the person to want to pursue whatever they are doing for its own sake. (From Flow: The Psychology of Optimal Experience, by Mihaly Csikszentmihalyi; Harper Perennial, 1991.)

Applying the Four-Stage Process

Application	HOME	HELP	CHALLENGE	PRIZE
Personal Development	• define your current situation • ask questions • create personal vision/mission • set goals • create standards/expecatations	• gather resources • get help, training, find a mentor, coach, counselor • develop skills • make a plan	• test yourself	• evaluate yourself • get feedback • go Home, begin again
Professional Development	• define your current situation • find out what's expected	• get necessary help • learn the required skills	• test your new skills	• evaluate yourself • get feedback • go Home, begin again
Leadership Development	• define your current situation • ask questions • create mission/vision • set goals • set standards/expectations	• give help • be a helper, role model, mentor, coach, sponsor • empower problem solving • provide skill development	• provide tests for others • maintain positive attitude • use positive influence	• assess results • give awards, rewards • go Home, begin again
Change Management	• define your current situation • ask questions	• get help, training • gather resources	• test and explore new policies, procedures, options, behaviors, feelings	• get feedback • evaulate new situation • go Home, begin again
Problem Solving	• define the problem • analyze possible causes	• generate possible solutions • select solution(s) • develop an action plan	• test your plan	• evaluate results • go Home, begin again
Flow	• define the situation • establish rules of "play" • create standards	• get training, education • gather resources	• test yourself	• get feedback • go Home, begin again
Team Building	• define your current situation • create mission/vision • set goals • assign roles • set standards	• get help, training, education • find a mentor, coach, counselor	• test yourself	• collect prizes • share rewards • go Home, begin again

Application	HOME	HELP	CHALLENGE	PRIZE
Risk Taking	• define your current situation • define goals/objectives	• get help/minimize risk • develop action plan	• test your plan	• evaluate results • go Home, begin again
Project Management	• define the project • set goals/objectives • define standards	• gather resources • assign roles • develop action plan	• test your plan	• evaluate results • go Home, begin again
Spiritual Evolution	• notice your current situation by hearing the "inner call" • accept the call to inner work	• find helpers, guidance • meditate	• break through barriers • confront your challenge	• gain inner connection • go Home, begin again
Heroic Transformation	• hear the call to adventure • prepare to leave	• find mentor, guides, helpers • learn the necessary skills	• test yourself, slay the "dragon"	• collect the treasure • go Home, share prizes, begin again
Scientific Methodology	• ask a question	• develop a theory	• test your theory	• reflect on what's been learned • go Home, begin again
Training Cycle	• define objectives • present overview content • present main points	• provide learning/content • provide supporting examples	• test and practice	• give/get feedback • go Home, begin again
Continuous Learning	• ask a question	• develop a theory	• test the theory	• reflect on what's been learned • get feedback • go Home, begin again

Multiplying Your Successes

Review the list of the 14 off-the-chart result categories and consider how many of these you experienced because of the success you described on the previous page. It is likely that you achieved more than you set out to, even if you didn't realize it. Check (✔) all the categories that apply to that success to remind yourself that achieving results is synergistic—the total success is greater than the sum of the individual effects.

- ❏ Personal development

- ❏ Professional development

- ❏ Leadership development

- ❏ Change management

- ❏ Problem solving

- ❏ Flow: the optimal experience

- ❏ Team building

- ❏ Risk taking

- ❏ Project management

- ❏ Spiritual evolution

- ❏ Heroic transformation

- ❏ Scientific methodology

- ❏ Training cycle

- ❏ Continuous learning

Tenets of Achieving Results

Note the following conclusions about achieving results:

➤ There are no guarantees in the process of achieving results.

➤ One person can make a difference.

➤ Most attempts at achieving results require confronting and overcoming obstacles.

➤ The more skilled you are, the greater the probability of the desired outcome.

➤ Intelligence comes in many forms, but it is not a predictor of favorable outcomes.

➤ All experiences offer lessons, which may be more valuable than the originally desired result.

➤ The more help you get (resources, time, money, training, suggestions, coaching, and so on), the greater the probability of achieving the outcome.

➤ The more clearly defined the desired result is, the more likely you are to achieve it.

➤ The length of time involved in arriving at outcomes is not a determinant of success.

➤ You can achieve multiple, synergistic, and positive results by using an effective process.

Factors Influencing Results

Results are influenced by many factors. Some of these factors are within your control; others are not. Add your own observations to this partial list:

Within Your Control	Out of Your Control
Attitude	Trends
Behaviors	Unforeseen crises
Participation	Weather
Thinking	Market volatility
Strategy	Natural disasters
Planning	Heredity
Others: _____	Others: _____
_____	_____

Five Criteria for Achieving Worthwhile Results

People and organizations are perfectly designed for the performance they achieve. You receive in proportion to what you give. If you want to put your resources into achieving results of value, consider the following five criteria:

Strategic: You need to have a plan. Results need to contribute to the mission, vision, and competitive advantage of an organization. Worthwhile results distinguish you from others and improve your "position" in the world.

Meaningful: This ensures that results are in alignment with core values and principles, thus providing a purpose or reason for achieving specific outcomes. Meaning also contributes to a sense of satisfaction and fulfillment.

Balanced: What you achieve in one area should not be gained (or lost) without considering its positive and/or negative impact in other areas.

Selfless: Selfless results create a greater good for all. Your results should benefit the whole in some way, not just one group or individual.

Enduring: Lasting results have residual value. If achieving a short-range result contributes in some way to a more enduring result, it becomes a means to a more valuable outcome.

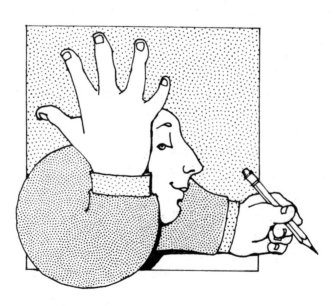

CASE STUDY: BOB

Bob earned a master's degree in business administration and immediately went to work in a factory. His plan was to start at ground zero and work his way into upper management. His hope was to eventually become CEO. He always saw himself as a leader, sitting in the corner office, and he wanted the independence that comes with calling the shots.

Within a few months, his hard work began to pay off; he was appointed team leader in his unit. He enjoyed the challenge and began reviewing what he had learned in college to create his career path. He created a personal mission statement, set goals, read the latest leadership books, enrolled in a "lean manufacturing" seminar, and asked for additional job responsibilities. Next, he created an action plan that he believed would catapult his career. This included observing a co-worker in management, Steve, as a role model. Bob respected Steve's judgment and believed that he could shorten his time to promotion by learning from others. He also decided that in order to qualify for management, he would need to improve his coaching skills and time management, show that he could implement lean manufacturing techniques within his team, and set ambitious work schedules. He began reading books on these subjects to gain the knowledge he needed.

When he began implementing his plan, however, his team members mistook his good intentions, viewing him as an aggressive corporate climber, only out for himself. Bob became discouraged with his early results and thought that if he couldn't effectively work with this small group of people, he would never be capable of running an entire company. He began to doubt that his desired long-range result of becoming CEO was right for him.

EVALUATING DESIRED RESULTS

Consider whether Bob's desired results are worthwhile by answering these questions.

What long-range result is Bob seeking? _____

Does Bob's desired result fit the five criteria for worthwhile results? Explain why or why not for each.

Strategic:

_____

_____

Meaningful:

_____

_____

Balanced:

_____

_____

Selfless:

_____

_____

Enduring:

_____

_____

CONTINUED

Compare your responses with the author's suggestions on page 12, then evaluate your own desired results against the five criteria.

CONTINUED

Does your desired result fit the criteria? In what way is your desired result:

Strategic:

_____

_____

Meaningful:

_____

_____

Balanced:

_____

_____

Selfless:

_____

_____

Enduring:

_____

_____

AUTHOR'S SUGGESTED ANSWERS

Bob's long-range result is to become a CEO.

His result is strategic because he had several plans that would enable him to advance his position and contribute to his overall mission.

Bob's result is meaningful because he values the outcome and believes it will contribute to a sense of satisfaction and fulfillment.

Bob needs improvement in balance because he focused too much on his own results without considering their effect on the morale of his staff.

Bob could use some improvement in creating selfless results. His motives appeared very self-serving to others. His desire to have independence and to "call the shots" did not consider the larger picture of how he would apply that power to a greater good. He wanted power for the sake of power, not for what that power could do to serve others. He needs to think about what he intends to do as a CEO (i.e., create more job opportunities, solve problems, invent something new).

Bob's result was enduring. His short-range goals created residual value by contributing to a long-range objective.

Summary Chart

Criteria	Questions	Clues to Problem	Proof of Success
Strategic	To what degree do my results align with strategies for my overall mission and vision of my personal life or organization?	Results are tied loosely or are nonexistent to strategies for business or life; results do not produce or add strategic focus or clarity	Results are tied strongly to business or personal life strategies
Meaningful	To what degree are my results aligned with core values and principles?	Results feel like busy-work, without "reason," and do not create a sense of importance or worth	Results create a sense of purpose, satisfaction, and fulfillment
Balanced	To what degree are my results balanced between organizational or personal result areas?	Results were aimed too much in one area, creating a negative impact in others	Results bring balance to the result areas and have a positive impact in others
Selfless	To what degree are my results selfless, creating benefits for the whole community and increasing capabilities without playing politics?	Results do not make the whole greater than the parts	Results support the entire organization or community and are not just for individual gain
Enduring	To what degree will the results last over time?	Results are for the short term and will not last—the "Band-Aid" approach	Results satisfy both short- and long-term goals and objectives

Off-the-Chart Results Assessment

This assessment involves answering 80 questions that reveal critical tasks in each of the four stages for reaching off-the-chart results. The italicized numbers identify the critical areas for organizational excellence as adapted from the 25-year Gallup Poll study of 80,000 managers in over 400 organizations.

Directions: Assess how you currently go about achieving results. Rate yourself on a scale of 1 to 5 and enter your answer in the appropriate space on the scorecard beginning on page 18.

5 = almost always   4 = usually   3 = average   2 = infrequently   1 = rarely

How often do you...

1. question old methods regarding how you go about achieving what you want?

2. feel that what you want has importance?

3. break down what you want into written goals?

4. know what is expected of you at work?

5. have the materials and equipment you need to accomplish the result?

6. take the opportunity to solve problems that affect your goals and responsibilities?

7. identify and develop critical skills needed to accomplish your goals?

8. turn your best guesses into theories about how you can get the result(s)?

9. focus on output (what you want), not on input?

10. know how and when to use persuasion as a tactic to get results?

11. see challenges as opportunities for personal and/or professional growth?

12. look for creative solutions if your plan needs modification?

Enter your results on the Scorecard, beginning on page 18.

13. have a feedback system to assess progress at all times in the process?

_____

14. receive praise or recognition for doing good work?

_____

15. see all experiences as learning experiences?

_____

16. feel gratitude when achieving goals?

_____

17. ask "why" questions when unclear about the purpose of what you want?

_____

18. recognize an opportunity to solve a problem or make a change?

_____

19. align goals and objectives in support of the organization's goals?

_____

20. have a way to measure outcomes?

_____

21. delegate responsibilites or tasks to free up time and energy?

_____

22. have the opportunity to do what you do best everyday?

_____

23. remain open to ideas, even though they have been tried before and didn't work?

_____

24. turn theories into written, stepped action plans with task deadlines?

_____

25. try to restrict or minimize fear from sabotaging your efforts?

_____

26. assertively ask for what you want without being aggressive?

_____

27. implement your plan once created without undue procrastination?

_____

28. use your intuitive intelligence to monitor and guide your action plan?

_____

29. measure and evaluate results against standards and expectations?

_____

30. consistently reward behaviors exceeding your plan?

_____

31. identify success traits of outputs and outcomes?

_____

32. enjoy each day?

_____

33. question your current situation to fully determine what's at stake?

_____

34. have a clear, written vision of the ideal future when the result is achieved?

_____

35. set realistic, achievable goals?

_____

36. set the bar for excellent, acceptable, and minimal outcomes?

_____

37. identify, gather, and utilize necessary information to achieve goals?

_____

38. feel that your opinion counts?

_____

39. remain teachable?

_____

40. identify who will do what and by when with the full agreement of all others involved?

_____

41. face tough challenges with optimism and a positive attitude?

_____

42. influence decision-making criteria when necessary or appropriate?

_____

43. keep your focus on the plan without getting distracted by lower priorities?

_____

44. use logical creativity techniques to solve problems?

_____

45. check the quality of your work before it leaves your area?

_____

46. sufficiently reward others involved in the process, either formally or informally?

_____

47. (in the last year) feel you had opportunites to learn and grow?

_____

48. feel that you have a best friend (at work)?

_____

49. ask questions to determine the root cause of the problem(s)?

_____

50. write a clear and concise mission in support of the vision?

_____

51. write down specifically what you will do each day to further your mission and vision?

_____

52. establish deadlines or cutoff points?

_____

53. have someone who encourages your development?

_____

54. speak up, confront issues, or disagree when necessary?

_____

55. continually learn to stretch your capabilities?

_____

56. have a contingency plan at the outset if "Plan A" fails?

_____

57. address setbacks quickly to get back on track without floundering?

_____

58. inspire yourself or others with enthusiasm?

_____

59. watch for indications that the plan is or is not working?

_____

60. recognize and resolve paradoxes?

_____

61. conduct ongoing, frequent, informal performance reviews?

_____

62. celebrate the result in some way, even if it's not what you had planned?

_____

63. recognize the unexpected wins?

_____

64. demonstrate that character is more important than total control?

_____

65. ask questions to identify roadblocks, inhibitors, and obstacles?

_____

66. establish culture and core values that align with the vision/mission?

_____

67. review your goals daily and make changes as necessary?

_____

68. feel that others involved are committed to quality work?

_____

69. feel that someone cares about you at work?

_____

70. feel respected as a person?

_____

71. develop your skills as a lifelong commitment to learning?

_____

72. modify the ineffective plans throughout the process if not on target?

_____

73. have the courage to face uncertainty?

_____

74. have the ability to lead others when necessary?

_____

75. have a way to monitor delayed results?

_____

76. take calculated risks?

_____

77. (over the last six months) have someone talk to you about your progress?

_____

78. provide merit rewards commensurate with achievement and behavior?

_____

79. have a way to direct poor performance?

_____

80. realize that success is measured by how many you serve, not by how many serve you?

_____

SCORECARD

Home				Help			
Question	Mission	Goals	Standards	Resources	Empower	Skills	Action Plan
1____	2____	3____	4____	5____	6____	7____	8____
17____	18____	19____	20____	21____	22____	23____	24____
33____	34____	35____	36____	37____	38____	39____	40____
49____	50____	51____	52____	53____	54____	55____	56____
65____	66____	67____	68____	69____	70____	71____	72____
Total	Total	Total	Total	Total	Total	Total	Total

Challenge				Prize			
Attitude Check	Influence	Monitor Plan	Creative Tinkering	Results	Rewards	Learning	Inner Wealth
9 _____	10 _____	11 _____	12 _____	13 _____	14 _____	15 _____	16 _____
25 _____	26 _____	27 _____	28 _____	29 _____	30 _____	31 _____	32 _____
41 _____	42 _____	43 _____	44 _____	45 _____	46 _____	47 _____	48 _____
57 _____	58 _____	59 _____	60 _____	61 _____	62 _____	63 _____	64 _____
73 _____	74 _____	75 _____	76 _____	77 _____	78 _____	79 _____	80 _____
Total	Total	Total	Total	Total	Total	Total	Total

Plotting Your Scores

Now total your scores for each column and plot them on the circular chart. If your score is beyond the boundary of the chart, then it is literally off-the-chart. That means you've reached a high level of proficiency or support in that area. If you score below 20 in a task, you've identified an area that may need development.

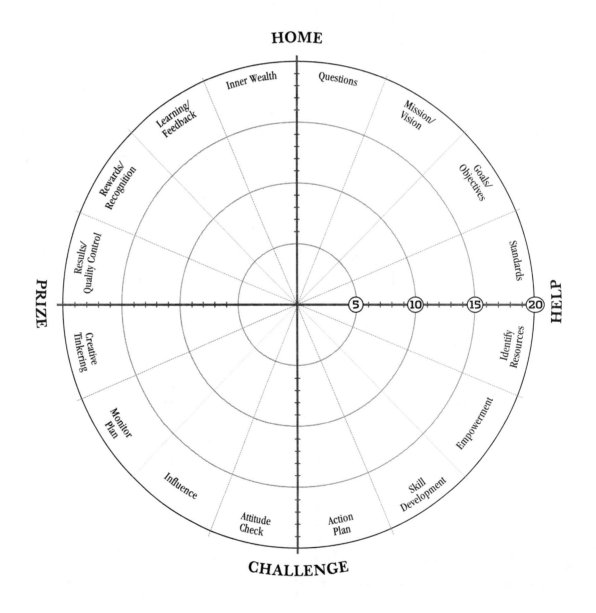

HOME

Inner Wealth   Questions

Learning/Feedback

Mission/Vision

Rewards/Recognition

Goals/Objectives

Results/Quality Control

Standards

PRIZE

⑤ ⑩ ⑮ ⑳

HELP

Creative Tinkering

Identify Resources

Monitor Plan

Empowerment

Influence

Skill Development

Attitude Check   Action Plan

CHALLENGE

Assessing Your "SWOT"

Now identify your *strengths, weaknesses, opportunities,* and *threats (SWOT)* for each stage of the process. This will help you to identify your basic tendencies when seeking to achieve results.

Using your scorecard, complete the following steps:

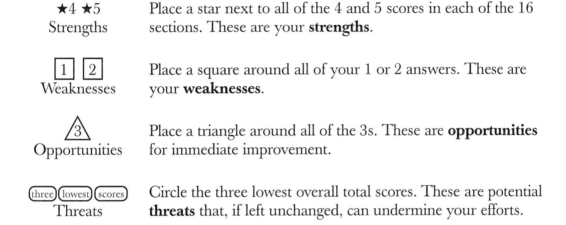

★4 ★5
Strengths

Place a star next to all of the 4 and 5 scores in each of the 16 sections. These are your **strengths**.

1   2
Weaknesses

Place a square around all of your 1 or 2 answers. These are your **weaknesses**.

△3
Opportunities

Place a triangle around all of the 3s. These are **opportunities** for immediate improvement.

(three)(lowest)(scores)
Threats

Circle the three lowest overall total scores. These are potential **threats** that, if left unchanged, can undermine your efforts.

Transfer all of your starred items (strengths) to the following SWOT chart. Enter the number of the assessment question, not your score, in the Strengths column next to the appropriate corresponding category.

Do the same for your squares (weaknesses), triangles (opportunities), and circles (threats). In this way, you have created a snapshot guide to your SWOT. This will assist you in creating a comprehensive strategic plan as you move forward.

Strengths	Weaknesses	Opportunities	Threats

Home–Deciding What You Want

"Our houses are such unwieldy property that we are often imprisoned rather than housed in them."

—Henry D. Thoreau

What Is Home?

Home is the starting place in the journey toward results. In order to achieve something, you must know what you want. Home helps define that desire. Home is also a metaphor for the habitual comfort zones we settle into—in our organizations, living arrangements, careers, relationships, or thinking.

Home provides two functions:

Rest and Rejuvenation: It's important to take a break from the rigors of life to regain one's balance from the stresses of too many changes and challenges. Stop and recharge at Home, while remembering that too much rest can be as destructive as no rest at all. You will know when to move on when the second function of Home begins to surface—a summons for change.

A Summons for Change: Home is also the starting point of the journey by defining what you want. Home disturbs our pattern of thinking out of complacency, by making a summons or request for change. It may come in very non-dramatic ways, so nontheatrical and quiet that we often miss its first attempts to get our attention. It could present itself as a small, quiet inner voice nagging at our conscious mind; some undefined restlessness; identification of a problem to be solved; or a grand mission. Requests for change may come from external sources such as other people or circumstances, or from your self. We typically respond to the summons for change in one of five ways:

> ➤ Ignoring the summons for change

> ➤ Willingly leaving Home

> ➤ Unwillingly leaving Home

> ➤ Unaware of leaving Home

> ➤ Indifferently leaving Home

Ignoring the Summons for Change

Sometimes we are asked to make changes but choose not to participate. Those who "rest" too long without responding to what's going on, however, can become victims of circumstance. In organizations, those who do not pay attention to their competitive situation will eventually be replaced by those who do.

Describe a situation in which you were asked to make a change but refused to participate.

_____

_____

_____

_____

Willingly Leaving Home

If you see a need to make changes and get results, you may leave Home to gain something new or to recover something that's been lost, in spite of the risk of leaving a comfort zone. There is no better time for change than when you or an organization is strong. Risk taking is safest when there's a cushion against failure. Starting a project, building profitability, or trying anything new may represent your willingness to make changes for the better.

List four situations in which you have willingly disrupted your comfort zone in search of something new, or to recover something that's been lost:

- _____

  _____

- _____

  _____

- _____

  _____

- _____

  _____

Unwillingly Leaving Home

Imagine yourself in a boat during a storm. The boat is rocking whether you want it to or not. Your comfort zone is now threatened by outside forces beyond your control—the death of a loved one, a market crash, changes in management, layoffs, or natural disasters. These are situations in which people are unwilling participants and are forced into change against their will.

List four situations in which you have been unwillingly thrown out of your comfort zone:

- _____

    _____

- _____

    _____

- _____

    _____

- _____

    _____

Unaware of Leaving Home

Being unaware of change is a form of denial, or choosing to ignore early danger signals. Sometimes we do not notice or respond to incremental clues of change—such as environmental toxins, illness, or economic shifts—before it's too late. By the time that the symptoms show up, the situation has escalated too far and sometimes it's irreversible.

List four situations in which you may have left Home unaware:

- _____

    _____

- _____

    _____

- _____
  _____

- _____
  _____

Indifferently Leaving Home

Indifference is a typical response of individuals who are constantly required to make changes and have become numb to the process. Constant reorganization, for example, can create employee apathy. People lose their ability to care because they've learned that their effort never has a payoff or has very little impact on short-term or long-term results.

List four situations in which you may have left Home indifferently:

- _____
  _____

- _____
  _____

- _____
  _____

- _____
  _____

Achieving Results Means Change

Change may be a means for solving problems, but change also presents challenges and risks because you are exchanging the known for the unknown. From the time you leave your comfort zone to the time of the result, you are in a state of transition. The success of your journey—from where you are to where you want to be—is determined by how well you move through and influence that transition.

Personal and organizational change involves transforming attitudes, behaviors, and processes into getting results. To change is to be in a continual process of growth toward some new destination, be it slow (evolutionary) or fast (revolutionary).

There are three roles you can play in the process of leaving Home and facing the challenges associated with change. Which of the following roles will you play in working toward your desired results?

❏ **Change Sponsor:** You have the authority to initiate the change, set the course, and be ultimately responsible for the result.

❏ **Change Agent:** You are responsible for implementing the change.

❏ **Change Target:** You are being asked to change an attitude, behavior, or approach as the means of implementing the change.

Dealing with the uncertainty of change often produces anxiety. While too much anxiety can be debilitating, we now know that a little stress can be a great motivator. A healthy response to fear can give us the adrenaline we need to initiate a running start.

On the other hand, when people are protected from challenge or failure, they expect to receive without having to achieve. Protecting people from challenges robs them of their self-esteem and opportunities to become fully functioning, competent, contributing human beings.

Without the exercise of change, challenge, and risk taking, people cannot learn how to face their challenges and push past them. These individuals never learn how to cope; therefore, ironically, "comfortable" people are overly cautious. When they should feel safe, they don't—because they've failed to develop their courage, confidence, and inner strength. The result of too much comfort and security, therefore, is the anxiety and paranoia about losing it.

Home Stage Tasks

There are four primary tasks to perform at Home as you begin the change process. They are listed in the most effective sequence, but we don't always have the luxury of performing tasks in a logical flow. You may find yourself skipping back and forth between the following tasks until they crystallize into your true mission.

➤ Asking questions

➤ Creating a vision and result mission

➤ Establishing goals

➤ Setting standards and expectations

These tasks have the added benefit of enabling you to let go of the past by identifying what you are giving up, what you will gain, and how you will know when you've arrived.

Asking Questions

Questions begin the quest, or search, for answers. They disturb our peace of mind and shift our thinking from *what is* to *what could be*. The most important question is, What do you want?

Over 2,300 years ago, Aristotle concluded that, more than anything else, people want happiness. Many things can do the job—recognition for a job well done, acquiring a new skill, buying an expensive car, a quiet moment of reflection. It doesn't have to be a mansion on a hill or a winning score. The definition is as varied as are the people who define it. It might be contributing to a worthwhile cause, solving a problem, or experiencing the simple joy of eating in a nice restaurant without worrying about the expense. Anything you want is ultimately the means to the result, and that is happiness. Many people work hard to find it, others hope to win it, others steal for it, some martyr themselves for it, and some wander aimlessly wondering what it is.

Do any of the following questions sound familiar?

"I'd be really good at something, *but what is it?"*

"I'm overworked and underpaid. Has life has passed me by?"

"Do I have what it takes to start my own business?"

"What's the problem here? My idea of happiness keeps changing."

"How can I complete my project on time and on budget?"

"Why is productivity down?"

"How can we improve the quality of our products and services?"

These are only a few of the questions we ask ourselves every day. Some of us think of these as problems or challenges. Others call them "opportunities." However we name them, these questions arise whenever there's a difference between where you are and where you'd like to be. They create gaps in our lives. Most of the time we're silent about it, living what Thoreau called a life of "quiet desperation," but sometimes it wells up and bursts on the scene in the form of divorce, job-hopping, broken relationships, or neurosis. It doesn't have to be that way.

Guidelines for Asking Questions

Begin your journey by asking yourself, What is my desired result?

Use the following five guidelines to help you pinpoint your answer:

> ➤ Create questions that identify what you really want

> ➤ Kill your internal editor

> ➤ Start from the general and lead to the specific

> ➤ Identify gaps in your life

> ➤ Take baby steps

1. **Create questions that identify what you really want.**

   Examples:

   > *What would I do if I knew I could not fail?*

   > *What would be the best possible outcome(s)?*

2. **Kill your internal editor.**

   Do not listen to the internal voice that says, "It's impossible," or "I could never do that." Answer questions boldly and with confidence, as if anything were possible.

3. **Start from the general and lead to the specific.**

   Answer as many of these questions as you can or come up with others that fit your situation.

   What do I want? _____

   _____

   When do I want it? _____

   _____

   How will I know when I have it? _____

   _____

   How will I go about achieving it? _____

   _____

What resources do I have that will help me achieve it? _____

_____

What skills do I need to learn? _____

_____

How can I increase my personal influence? _____

_____

How will I track my progress? _____

_____

What will be my reward? _____

_____

Who else will benefit? _____

_____

Additional Questions to Pinpoint Desired Results:

What project do you want to complete?

What problem needs to be solved?

What would you like to have happen in your life?

What relationship would you like to improve?

What are your unfulfilled goals?

What angers you most?

What misunderstandings exist?

What would you like others to do?

What do you wish you had more time to do?

What changes would you like to implement?

What takes too long or wears you out?

What is too complicated?

Where are the obstacles and bottlenecks?

4. **Identify gaps in your life.**

We have all felt gaps in our lives—those vague (or not-so-vague) discomforts that point to a discrepancy between where we are and where we want to be. Identifying the discomfort in your life gives birth to the desire and opportunity to eliminate that pain. If you're frustrated over a job, for example, that frustration creates a gap and a clue about the work conditions that you don't want. If you decide to do something about it, you've just made a move toward your success—what you do want. The problem is solved when you close the gap between where you are and where you want to be.

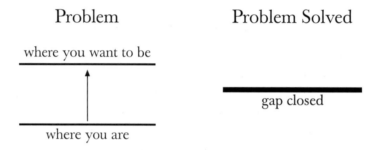

5. **Take baby steps.**

Think big, but move in increments. The more narrowly defined your desired result is, and the shorter the time for its accomplishment, the easier it is to control, manage, and measure. Take baby steps; this policy of incrementalism will gradually resolve small hurdles, which adds up to bigger accomplishments. Grandiose or complex results occur after a series of hundreds, or even thousands, of incremental baby-step results.

Before you move on, try to answer as many questions as possible regarding your desired result. But if you don't have answers yet, don't worry. The journey itself is designed to provide answers.

Home Creating a Vision and Result Mission

Questions stimulate thinking, but creating a vision and a result mission generate excitement about the possibilities to come and keep the project going when energy begins to wane. Ideally, your vision statement should be written down, communicated, and made accessible to all involved.

Creating a Vision Statement: The Power of "Seeing" Results

A vision statement is a written account, or mental picture, of what your ideal result looks like. Creating a vision statement is like capturing a snapshot of the way you envision the future. Writing down specifics enables you to clarify your goals, making the vague clear. Studies show that many top performers have the ability to see their successes before they happen.

Florence Chadwick was the first woman to swim the English Channel in both directions. Following this feat, her subsequent goal was to be the first woman to swim from Catalina Island to the California coast. On the morning of July 4, 1952, the icy, shark-infested waters were covered with a fog so dense she could not see her support boats. Millions watched on national television.

After swimming for 16 numbing hours and with only half a mile to go, she decided to quit, despite the encouragement of her mother and trainer. Hours later, while still thawing her chilled body, she told a reporter, "Look, I'm not excusing myself, but if I could have seen the land, I might have made it." Neither fatigue nor the cold water defeated her—she could not see her goal.

Two months later she tried again under similar circumstances, and this time she made it. With a vision of what she wanted clearly pictured in mind and her positive expectation that she could do it, she became the first woman to swim the Catalina Channel, beating the men's record by two hours!

Guidelines for Creating a Vision Statement

To create an effective vision statement, observe the following four guidelines:

➤ Write it down.

➤ Word it as though the result is already achieved.

➤ Include specific actions.

➤ Provide enough detail to make it seem plausible.

The following is a sample vision statement that needs improvement:

"I want to build a successful national sales team that consistently surpasses the competition. I'd like the team to win the prestigious Davis Award for industry professionalism. My team will share their best ideas with one another."

Let's analyze the preceding statement against the four criteria.

➣ **Is it written down?**
Yes.

➣ **Is it worded as though the result is already achieved?**
No, it is worded as a desire, not a fact. "I want to build...", "I'd like the team to win...," and "My team will share..." indicate unmet desires. Consider these revised alternatives: "We have a successful national sales team..."; "Our team won..."; and "My team shares..." You can see the powerful difference a little wording makes.

➣ **Does it include specific actions?**
No, it does not include specific actions. The author of this statement could add some of the ways in which the team surpasses the competition, such as through fast turn-around time, Internet commerce, and customer partnership strategies. He or she could also add any actions that would lead to winning the coveted award, such as increased customer contact, follow-through procedures, and team selling.

➣ **Does it provide enough detail to make it seem plausible?**
No, it needs more detail. The author could add some of the details suggested above. He or she might also add, as examples, sharing best ideas at weekly meetings and naming top competitors.

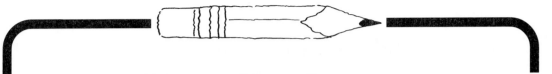

WRITING A VISION STATEMENT

An improved version helps to "see" more of the future:

"I have a successful national sales team that consistently outproduces our top five competitors through fast turn-around time, Internet traffic, and customer "partnering" strategies. Our increased customer contact, follow-through procedures, and team selling have won us the prestigious Davis Award for industry professionalism. My team sets the standard for excellence by sharing their best ideas with one another at weekly meetings and through a spirit of cooperation."

Write your own vision statement, regardless of any obstacles that may currently stand in your way. Use more paper if you need to.

_____

_____

_____

_____

_____

_____

_____

_____

_____

_____

_____

_____

_____

_____

Creating a "Result" Mission Statement

A mission is a statement of purpose. It specifies the *means* to an end, such as "protect and serve," "end the war," or "be the best." It is a special assignment for a person or a group that will contribute to the creation of the vision. If vision is the future looking back to the present, then missions are the present looking forward to the future. A *result* mission statement, however, is not only a statement of the means to the end; it also defines the true *desired result of the mission*. This is accomplished by attaching two simple words: "so that."

Mission: To meet the changing needs of our customers

Result Mission: To meet the changing needs of our customers, *so that* they will continue doing business with our company

The mission is to be flexible with customers, but the real desired *result* of the mission is to ensure continued business success.

Result missions keep personal and organizational focus in alignment with the vision and help people direct efforts that support what they're *really* going after, not just the means with which to do so.

Guidelines for Creating a Result Mission Statement

There are also four guidelines for creating an effective result mission statement:

➤ It should be no longer than a phrase or sentence.

➤ Include the words "so that."

➤ Include at least one verb.

➤ Imply benefit to others as well as to the individual.

Writing Result Mission Statements

Practice writing result mission statements. Make up a desired result for each of the following examples.

Mission	Desired end result
CEO	Become a world-class leader so that...
Writer	Write a best-selling novel so that...
Sales manager	Build a world-class team so that...

Now write your own "result" mission statement, including the words "so that."

_____

_____

_____

_____

_____

_____

_____

_____

_____

_____

Establishing Goals

Your vision and result mission now need to be converted into goals. Goals define the efforts needed to successfully complete the vision and mission, while reflecting personal or organizational culture and values. Think of goals as incremental results, or "baby steps," needed to achieve the mission. They are like letters of the alphabet—they can stand alone with a single purpose, but they can also be part of something much larger and more meaningful. Large goals provide general organizational guidance, while more modest, specific goals get the detailed tasks done. There are three levels of organizational goals:

Organizational Level	Goal Example
Operational goal	Increase revenue 10% by year-end
Departmental goal	Hire 12 new sales executives
Individual goal	Open one new account each week

Goal achievement is like reaching a summit. A summit is the highest level or degree that can be attained—in this case, your vision and mission. Following are six criteria for setting effective SUMMIT goals.

Goals should be:

S pecific and written:
Write down specific actions needed to complete your mission

U nderstandable:
They should be clear enough to communicate to others without misinterpretation

M easurable:
Define how you will know if you've achieved your goal

M anageable:
You should be realistically able to control the necessary tasks

I deal:
Specify the ideal realistic outcome

T ime-sensitive:
Specify a date when the goal is to be achieved

Examples

Result Mission: Build global awareness of nonviolent solutions to international conflict in order to reduce arms build-up and warfare.

Goals: Join the Peace Corps at the end of my senior year in college.

     Establish the World Federation of Peace Studies Institute by 2010.

Result Mission: Win Best New Car Design Award so that our company and shareholders will prosper.

Goals: Complete new car concept within 10 months.

     Install new brake technology in next season's models.

WRITING EFFECTIVE GOALS

Is the following a SUMMIT goal? Refer to the preceding list and check off those criteria it satisfies.

"The goal is to reduce absenteeism in my department by 50% by Jan. 1, 2010, without exceeding the annual employee recognition budget of 7K."

Compare your answers to those of the author on the next page.

Author's Answers

S = Yes, it is specific and written down.

U = Yes, it is understandable.

M = Yes, the result can be measured by a drop in absenteeism (50%), by a due date (Jan. 1), and by a budget (7K).

M = Yes, the author of the statement believes it is manageable because the plan can be broken into parts.

I = Yes, this is an ideal realistic outcome.

T = Yes, it has a due date for the goal.

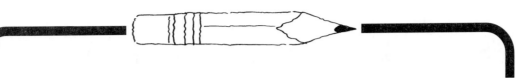

SETTING YOUR OWN GOALS

Write your own goals for your result mission, and then put them in chrono-
logical order. If you're not sure of all the goals needed to achieve the result,
try working backward from the result to the present. What would have to
happen right before the result? Before that? Use the following worksheet to
help your planning.

	Goals	Measured Results	Due Date
1.			
2.			
3.			
4.			
5.			
6.			
7.			
8.			
9.			
10.			

Note: The more you involve the appropriate members of your organization
in the goal-setting and planning process, the greater their buy-in and motivation for making the goal(s) a reality.

Setting Standards and Expectations

If you want to avoid wasted time, effort, and disappointment, create standards and expectations for your results. These define who will do the specific activities needed to achieve the goals, and what level of quality you are looking for in your result. What is your measurement of success or failure? What is excellent, acceptable, and unacceptable? A common complaint of employees is that they simply don't know what's expected. Without clearly defined expectations, people are left guessing; and often, they guess wrong.

Standards are levels of requirement that measure quantitative or qualitative values. They "set the bar" for organizational practices, and they establish the criteria for measuring tangibles, intangibles, levels of service, and quality. They also relate to softer issues such as values, ethics, culture, and philosophies. Setting standards requires a search for the best internal or external practices and using them as a measurement stick for others to follow and improve on. The best time to develop standards and measures is when a goal or project is first approved.

The Benefits of Setting Standards

Setting standards and sharing them with all involved will help you:

➤ Consistently meet and exceed the wants and needs of customers or others involved

➤ Improve performance capabilities and practices

➤ Recognize when expected outcomes or targets have been achieved

➤ Manage the performance, planning, training, and assessment of outcomes

➤ Create best-in-class behaviors and outcomes by using the best performers as models

➤ Build a continuous learning organization through feedback and evaluation

➤ Save time and money by cutting down on trial and error

➤ Validate goals and their alignment with current needs or market trends

➤ Create controlled rapid growth instead of incremental growth

➤ Keep everyone on track by letting them know where they stand

To be effective in organizations, standards should have clearly established objectives based on requirements such as product design, customer service response time, and project schedules. In a personal situation, standards need to define the criteria by which you will measure your success. If your desired result is to get a satisfying job, define your criteria. What is satisfying to you? What kind of work would you most want to do? What pay is acceptable or outstanding? What benefits are expected or needed? You get what you measure, so measure what you want.

Here are three ways of getting started setting standards for a project or initiative within an organization:

➤ Conduct surveys and polls to find out how well your products or services align with the needs of your customers, and create goals that satisfy those demands.

➤ Enlist appropriate individuals in writing job descriptions and establishing roles, responsibilities, and standards for the project. In this way, you enlist greater support and benefit from many points of view and experience. Communicate roles and job assignments to others so that people will understand lines of responsibility.

➤ Identify performance standards and expectations that define your levels of quality. Be specific in identifying minimal, satisfactory, and outstanding criteria for measuring success. In times of crisis, people need to know their boundaries in order to make sound decisions.

For personal results, standards should be based on your specific requirements, both short-term and long-term; and consider the needs of others affected by your desired results. For example, if you are seeking wellness as a result, what level of wellness do you seek? Getting out of bed? Running a marathon? Stopping the pain? If you want to start a business, how will you define it as successful? When will you have reached that point of your desired result? When you get your business license? Your first dollar? Your first million dollars?

U se the worksheet on the next page to set standards that will help you realize when you have truly achieved your desired results.

ESTABLISHING YOUR CRITERIA FOR SUCCESS

Define standards and expectations for your goals. Set minimal, acceptable, and outstanding criteria for measuring the results. If others are involved, be sure to communicate the criteria to them so that everyone knows what's expected. Ensure that you have the willing compliance of others, revising your standards if necessary.

Goal: _____

Standards and Expectations:

    Minimum: _____

    Acceptable: _____

    Outstanding: _____

Goal: _____

Standards and Expectations:

    Minimum: _____

    Acceptable: _____

    Outstanding: _____

Goal: _____

Standards and Expectations:

    Minimum: _____

    Acceptable: _____

    Outstanding: _____

Goal: _____

Standards and Expectations:

    Minimum: _____

    Acceptable: _____

    Outstanding: _____

Help–Getting Help and Creating an Action Plan

> *"The only sustainable competitive advantage in business today is the ability to learn faster."*
>
> —Peter Senge, *The Fifth Discipline*

What Is Help?

The Home stage identifies *what* you want. Help defines *how* best to achieve it. Help is perhaps the most important stage of the four, yet often the most overlooked or underutilized. Most plans fail because of inadequate or inappropriate help. Getting the right kind of help can make the difference between success and failure.

The benefits of the Help stage are critical to your success. From the following list, check (✔) the benefits that are most important to you:

❏ Increase personal capacity and capabilities through learning and targeted assistance

❏ Promote confidence through increased competence

❏ Stimulate alternative solutions to problems

❏ Speed up the process of getting results

❏ Reduce guesswork, mistakes, and errors

❏ Shorten learning time

❏ Build personal and organizational unity by communicating common goals

❏ Build a climate of innovation through the sharing of knowledge and information

❏ Increase productivity through enhanced skills

❏ Increase team effectiveness and delegation capabilities through cross-training

Before you can get all the help you need, you must assume responsibility for knowing what you need. Is it a name, a telephone number, a book, an account, a skill, a support network? Do you need to talk to a person, set up a meeting, or get a tool? Being specific about what you need is one of the first steps in the Help stage toward making your results a reality.

Guidelines for Getting Help

Following are some guidelines for getting the right kind of help. Think of your desired result and check it against these criteria.

Help should:

➤ "feel" right—listen to your gut

➤ not endanger life or safety

➤ be verifiable, if possible

➤ be reputable

➤ be time-tested, if possible

➤ be field-tested, if possible

➤ be experienced

➤ be well-practiced

➤ be cross-checked with other opinions

➤ be researched

➤ come from several sources

➤ be current, if appropriate

➤ align with basic moral and value systems

➤ maximize strengths and minimize weaknesses

➤ be well-organized

➤ be thorough

➤ involve those who have expertise in your area of focus

➤ be innovative, if appropriate

➤ use common sense

➤ be targeted toward your desired result

Help Stage Tasks

There are infinite ways of getting help, but they can be organized into four distinct tasks that will move you toward your desired result:

➤ Identifying resources

➤ Getting empowered

➤ Developing skills

➤ Creating an action plan

Identifying Resources

A resource is anything or anyone that offers support or help. Resources represent the tools available for getting things done, such as people, money, materials, equipment, buildings, information, and any other fixed or liquid assets. There are three main categories of resources: human, informational, and miscellaneous.

Human Resources

Human resources are people who can provide guidance, expertise, and support, such as mentors, role models, teachers, coaches, counselors, delegates, assistants, friends, and relatives.

The human resources Bob sought were his college professors, his lean manufacturing instructor, and his co-worker Steve. Bob might have gained more valuable insight if Steve had been assigned as an "official" mentor or coach. In this way, he could have learned more about Steve's motivations and resulting actions.

What human resources help will *you* complete your mission?

_____

_____

Informational Resources

Professor Stephen Hawking believes that the greatest innovation of the past millennium was the printing press. The transfer of information was catapulted into warp speed. Information resources are those that give us access to research, data, information technology, or any other knowledge that can shed light on the best ways to achieve the results we seek.

Bob used books as his primary informational resource—in subjects such as coaching skills, time management, lean manufacturing, and scheduling. Other information resources include the Internet, professional associations, seminars, workshops and presentations, videos and other media.

What informational resources will help you?

_____

_____

Miscellaneous Resources

Miscellaneous resources include anything else that provides support or help, such as tools, equipment, and fixed or liquid assets.

Bob's miscellaneous resources were the additional job responsibilities he sought to increase his job experience.

What other resources will you need?

_____

_____

Help Getting Empowered

It is difficult to get results without some level of personal power, called *empowerment*. This is the degree of authority you hold in making decisions, planning, developing skills, informing, monitoring progress, motivating, rewarding, evaluating, solving problems, and establishing policy. You can be both empowering (extending power to others) and empowered (having the authority to act). Empowerment determines how much effect you have in helping yourself and others achieve goals and objectives. Check (✔) those areas in which you are currently empowered.

I am empowered to:

- ❏ improve or create action plans

- ❏ make decisions to solve problems

- ❏ inform others

- ❏ monitor progress of the entire project or parts of the project

- ❏ motivate others to act

- ❏ reward effort and results

- ❏ do the right things, instead of just doing things right

- ❏ take responsibility for solving problems

- ❏ take initiative, rather than waiting for direction

- ❏ work within quality parameters to achieve organizational results beyond average requirements

- ❏ improve processes in addition to results

- ❏ speak up, take risks, and take action

Within organizations, management's role is to provide help in the form of necessary resources, guidelines, and plans, while holding people accountable for getting results. Empowering others does not mean giving up control; it frees management's time to be better managers, which helps managers have a wider span of control and accomplish more through others.

The Benefits of Empowerment

The benefits of being an empowered individual or workforce are numerous. Following are just a few of the additional benefits gained through empowerment. Check (✔) those that are most critical to your results:

- ❏ Sharing knowledge and information

- ❏ Cooperative partnerships versus individual territories

- ❏ Customer-focused problem solving

- ❏ True power (the real ability to inspire and produce, not the power of a title)

- ❏ Positive morale

- ❏ Clear communication

- ❏ Meaningful rewards and recognition

- ❏ Cooperative team work

The Ritz-Carlton Hotel chains have empowered their employees with expenditures of up to $2,500 to resolve any guest problems. This enables employees to quickly resolve on-the-spot issues without tying up operations.

The best service strategies include the following two factors:

➤ Staff is empowered at the point of service

➤ Staff is empowered to resolve issues

No one knows a job better than the person who performs it. Who better to make decisions and solve on-the-spot problems than the expert? Once an individual is given the freedom to work within this system for creating the best output, untold innovation and creative problem solving emerges.

Bob was an empowered employee because he asked for additional job responsibilities that would increase his job experience. He spoke up, took risks, and took action. He created action plans, made decisions to solve problems, monitored progress, and took the initiative, rather than waiting for directions. However, he could have empowered his staff to do more. This would have given them the opportunity to participate and be part of the organization's success, rather than feeling Bob was only interested in personal gain.

Developing Skills

Consider the meaning of the following sentence:

People pay for training and education whether they invest in it or not.

Individuals and organizations pay for lack of skill development, education, and training—in lost opportunities, lost revenue, missed deadlines, poor service, reduced customer base, mistakes, and much more. The fact is that we always pay for education and training, one way or another.

Skills can be categorized into two types:

➤ **Hard skills** refer to tasks such as filling out paperwork, processing a report, or running a machine.

➤ **Soft skills** refer to tasks that help you to do the job through non-tangibles, such as interpersonal communication, time management, problem solving, and decision-making.

Make a list of the hard and soft skills needed to reach the results you are seeking.

Hard Skills	Soft Skills

Creating an Action Plan

Now it's time to put everything from the Home and Help stages together into a comprehensive action plan. This puts the *what* and *when* with the *who* and *how*. The function of the action plan is twofold:

Forecast: Set objectives, strategies, and tactics; establish budgets, policy, and procedure; troubleshoot obstacles.

Organize: Create order out of the tasks that have been accumulating; identify the detail work to be done and who will do it. Delegate responsibilities; set up working relationships between all those involved.

The action plan is a dynamic document that is subject to change, depending on outcomes and unplanned influences. At this point, it's your best guess, or theory, about how to proceed from here. Keep in mind: *There is no perfect plan!*

Strive for improvement, not perfection. The variables of competition, economic fluctuations, technological advances, consumer loyalties, government policy, media influence, your readiness, and more, can and will disrupt even the most carefully calculated plans. Therefore, an action plan is, at best, nothing more than an organized theory about how you think you can bring about the desired result.

Consider where you are and allow for the following variables:

➤ Individual or customer wants and needs

➤ Availability of resources (human, information, assets, energy)

➤ Current trends such as markets, buying interests, and fads

➤ Local, national, and world economic outlook

➤ Regulatory and political developments

➤ Changes in policy

➤ Investor expectations

➤ Competitive trends

DOCUMENTING YOUR PLANS

Many powerful action-planning tools are available today, particularly as computer software.

Following are a few examples of how to organize information for your action plan.

Key Tasks	Skills Required	Person(s) Assigned	Start Date	Due Date	Desired Results

A daily planner sample

Top Priority Tasks		
❑ 1.		
❑ 2.		
❑ 3.		
❑ 4.		
❑ 5.		
Tasks	**Priority Rank**	**Time**
❑ Meet		
❑ Call		
❑ Write		
❑ Plan		
❑ Analyze		

Troubleshooting Your Action Plan

An important part of the planning stage is troubleshooting. This means considering what could go wrong, modifying the plan if necessary, and building contingency plans. Troubleshooting can be as simple as asking and answering three questions:

"What can go wrong?"

"How can it be prevented?"

"How can it be fixed if it happens?"

The extent of your need to troubleshoot will depend upon the complexity of your action plan. It is useful to have troubleshooting done by people other than those who created the action plan. This provides a fresh perspective that may uncover more problems and/or solutions.

Here are five approaches to troubleshooting:

➤ Conducting a critical review

➤ Predicting results

➤ Testing

➤ Exemplifying

➤ Exaggerating

Conducting a Critical Review

Conducting a critical review means asking and answering critical questions about your plan. Sometimes people don't know which questions will reveal weaknesses in their plan. Following are some examples you may use for your own desired result:

1. Why are you going for the result? What will be gained?

2. What is the probability that the proposed plan will achieve the objectives?

3. What are the drawbacks or disadvantages of the plan?

4. Does anything in this plan make you uneasy? If so, what?

5. Who or what might sabotage the plan?

6. Will the action plan cause embarrassment to anyone (such as management, customers, employees, the community, or other departments)?

7. How will you communicate the plan in sufficient detail to gain support from others and clarify your expectations?

8. Are there adequate personnel to implement and carry out the plan?

9. Are the goals and objectives of the plan desirable, sound, and understood?

10. Is the time frame realistic?

11. Is there a better time to implement the plan?

12. What are the circumstances or conditions that could affect your time frame?

13. What can you do about them?

14. Is there a better way to pursue the plan?

15. Who else needs to be included in the approval process or be informed about the decision?

16. Is the plan cost-efficient? Have you cut needless spending without compromising the quality you're after?

If you act on your answers every time you conduct a critical review, 25% to 50% of problems could be eliminated before they occur. Be proactive, not reactive.

Predicting Results

Estimate the most likely consequences of the actions being planned, and then adjust the plan as needed to increase the probability of positive results. Predicting results enables you to qualify and quantify both positive and negative outcomes. Since no one has a crystal ball, you may wish to create a backup plan as insurance just in case you miscalculate the outcomes.

CASE STUDY: CAROL

Carol has a mission. She would like to return to school to get her master's degree in marketing so that she will be eligible to manage her department someday. The company she works for is growing rapidly; it promotes from within, and it reimburses employees for educational classes. Carol faces challenges to her plan. She is a single mother of two with a full-time job and limited funds, and she has serious doubts that she can pull it off.

Carol wants to "predict" her success for getting her master's degree. Her analysis is outlined in a chart on the next page.

The chart helped Carol identify obstacles to her goal. She guesstimated the probability of occurrence of each problem and gave it a percentage value. By identifying the importance of the impact for each problem, she recognized where she needed to amend the plan. If the potential problem was of little consequence, she may have chosen to simply acknowledge it and move on.

Carol predicts that she will be successful in achieving her result because of sound planning. She has decided to test Plan A for one semester. She estimates that she can take two classes per semester and will graduate in four years. If Plan A fails, she will move to Plan B and try another combination of strategies to see what will work best.

Predict the probability of your result success by identifying potential problems and what you can do to offset their impact.

Carol's Analysis

Potential Problems	Estimated Probability of Occurence	Importance of Impact 1-10	Actions to Increase Positive Results	Contingency Plan B (Actions if Plan A Fails)
• Not enough time with kids	100%	10	• More quality time during the day; put kids in daycare close to work; have lunch together • Special weekend activities	• Hire someone to come into home for daycare - or - • Quit job; live on low-interest loans; finish in two years
• Fatigue	100%	9	• Eat high-energy food: veggies, fruit, no junk • Exercise with kids	• Take ginseng and vitamins; no coffee - or - • Shorter workday - or - • Flextime workweek
• Lose interest and drop out; self-doubt	50%	10	• Focus on payoffs: increased pay, better lifestyle, college money for kids	• Find a coach at work who will encourage me

Testing

This approach enables you to save time and money, reduce risk, and test the effectiveness of the plan through the use of "safe" environments. These include models, study groups, focus groups, controlled conditions, and representative samplings.

Test results can then be extended to larger areas that will be affected by the plan. Fairly reliable decisions about a course of action can then be made regarding feasibility and potential problems.

A note of caution: Make sure that the data tests the actual variables being considered. To do so, it is best to limit the number of factors being tested (to increase control of the data) and to include all the details.

Example:

> *If you are testing the popularity of gym equipment, do not overlook the temperature in the room, the availability of water, the wall color, lighting, and so on. Each of these variables affects the user's impression.*

How might you test your plan before implementation? Check (✔) those that are appropriate for your result:

❑ **Models:** Create a model of what you are doing to test for structure, design, color, flow, and so on.

❑ **Study groups:** Assign a group to study the plan, discuss options, and run a feasibility study.

❑ **Focus groups:** Gather a group of people to discuss the plan and offer feedback.

❑ **Controlled conditions:** Set up a mock test of the plan using a tightly controlled environment.

❑ **Representative samplings:** Take samples from select groups of people to get feedback.

Exemplifying

Exemplifying means evaluating specific examples of situations that will most likely be encountered when the plan is implemented. This enables you to pinpoint potential problems and opportunities before they occur.

Example:

If you are considering implementing a new company-wide policy, consider how the plan might affect operations in different areas of the organization. Ask how the new policy would affect employees in accounting, sales, marketing, R & D, and so on.

How might you use exemplifying to troubleshoot your plan?

_____

_____

Exaggerating

Exaggerating is blowing the impact of the plan out of proportion. Overstating the most likely consequences encourages new perspectives and deeper thinking in creating more effective contingency plans and alternatives.

Example:

"What's the worst thing that can happen? The best?"

How might you use exaggerating to troubleshoot your plan?

_____

_____

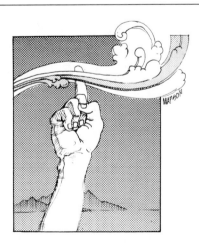

Action Planning Checklist

Use the following steps to put your working plan or "theory" together. Check off each item as you complete it.

❑ List goals and objectives that support the mission and vision.

❑ Outline major tasks for each goal.

❑ Break major tasks into detailed tasks.

❑ Determine the best case, the worst case, and the expected start and completion dates.

❑ Estimate resource requirements.

❑ Determine all resources needed to begin a task.

❑ Gather resources, including tracking charts and graphs.

❑ Incorporate strategies, tactics, and troubleshooting.

❑ If others are involved, distribute the plan and discuss with all parties involved.

❑ Fine-tune and issue the final plan.

Challenge–
Testing the Plan

"When you're going through hell, keep going."

—Winston Churchill

What Is Challenge?

The challenge stage involves implementing your plan, facing a test, solving a problem, or confronting a difficulty that must be resolved before the result can be achieved. It is the "moment of truth," sometimes called *dragon slaying*, when the theory you've created is tested for its effectiveness. The challenge is the point at which change takes place, and change can be messy.

Challenges are, by definition, difficult. However, there is a difference between the difficulty of a challenge and our emotional uneasiness about it. Emotions provide important clues that can guide the way if we listen hard and long enough to hear the message. Good judgment and common sense go a long way toward negotiating dark waters. Do not ignore the sensation of needing "a bigger boat" if you think you're in over your head. "If a project feels uncomfortable, then something's probably wrong," says experienced project manager Bill Drobny. The trick in the challenge stage is having the wisdom to know the difference between the difficulty of hard work and things that feel wrong.

When working through a challenge, something must change in order for you to emerge on the other side. This means giving up some part of the past and letting go of the known. You have to give up something (the status quo) to get something (the desired result). Challenges are not simply obstacles. They are also opportunities. Focus on the opportunity to solve problems and you'll find joy in challenges.

CASE STUDY: SAM

Sam has been asked to be the lead manager on a new project that needs completion in one month. He's not sure how the project fits into the company mission, but he can choose anyone he wants to help him get it done. Unfortunately, there is no budget. This project is not part of anyone's job responsibilities, and Sam has no authority over other managers in allocating employee time.

As shown in the following chart, Sam will run into many of the challenges typical to achieving off-the-chart results. Indicate which challenges you think you will run into as you work toward your desired result.

Sam's Challenges

Typical Challenges	Challenges Sam Will Encounter	Challenges You Anticipate Encountering
Participating in a contest or competition		
Engaging in conflict, confrontation, or a fight		
Entering new territory or the unknown	new project	
Calling for an explanation or justification; a calling into question	unsure of project purpose	
Testing one's abilities or resources in a demanding but stimulating undertaking	few resources; tight deadline	
Claiming that a vote is invalid or that a voter is unqualified		
Formally objecting to the inclusion of a prospective juror in a jury		
Testing attributes, qualifications, identity, or response	attributes of co-workers will be tested	
Testing the status quo	adding to existing workload	
Testing the efficacy or validity of something		
A summons to action, effort, or use	request to complete a new project	
Psychological, attitudinal, or mental struggles	potential mental stress from increased workload	
Time and money shortages	tight deadline; no budget allocated	
Uncooperative co-workers	potential due to increased workload	
No influence over others	level of authority not increased	

Obstacles

Challenges can be classified in two ways:

External: These are challenges that come from circumstances outside of us, such as natural disasters, crisis, chaos, a new job, getting married, being drafted by the military, or giving a presentation. In organizations, external challenges that prevent the actual work from taking place are called *performance obstacles*.

Internal: These are challenges that we confront psychologically, including fear, doubt, low self-esteem, anger, lack of motivation, negative self-talk, or any issues that sour attitude and prevent the project from moving forward. Internal obstacles within organizations are called *satisfaction obstacles*.

You will find many of Sam's obstacles in the following list. Check (✔) any obstacles that may stand in your way.

Performance Obstacles

❑ boring work

❑ lack of authority to make changes

❑ red tape

❑ uncooperative staff

❑ inadequate training or skills

❑ too many conflicting priorities

❑ inefficiency and work bottlenecks

❑ incorrect/incomplete work from others

❑ too much work for time allotted

❑ interruptions

❑ inadequate communication systems

❑ conflicting interdepartmental goals

❑ other:

Satisfaction Obstacles

❑ routine work

❑ overcriticized

❑ rewarded with more work

❑ someone else gets the credit

❑ importance of work not clear

❑ apathetic management

❑ inconsistent or no rewards

❑ work not important to you

❑ can't see end result(s)

❑ too many changes in direction

❑ too much confusion

❑ empowerment not "real"

❑ other:

Each of these obstacles presents an opportunity to fix a problem. Consider how you might work through each one to achieve your desired result. Ask others to help you with ideas and support.

Challenge Stage Tasks

There are four main tasks at the challenge stage:

➤ Checking Your Attitude. Maintain an effective, appropriate frame of mind to work through the challenge(s).

➤ Increasing Your Influence. Increase your power to affect circumstances or other people.

➤ Testing and Monitoring the Plan. Keep track of the action plan or project's progress to be sure you're on track.

➤ Creatively Tinkering. Exercise your creativity to experiment and innovate, or to explore possibilities when the path is unclear.

Checking Your Attitude

A large body of literature supports the power of maintaining a positive attitude. It energizes, inspires, brings out the best in people, strengthens the immune system, and keeps projects alive when the going gets tough. The nature of the Challenge stage is that it not only tests the plan, but tests the psychological inner world of the individual as well.

The internal struggle we confront in our mind is often the greatest challenge of all. Instinctively, we know that the journey toward results is a journey toward self-discovery. It teaches us who we are, forms our character, and tests our inner fortitude. Achieving results, then, is ultimately a test of the individual, and many are not up to the task. We are often our own worst enemy because of inappropriate attitude.

Attitudes are a state of mind, or emotions, that form our disposition. Some individuals are lucky enough to be born with a naturally positive, upbeat disposition. Much of our attitude is based on our chemistry. Thankfully, we can change that chemistry by changing our behavior. For example, physical movement (exercise) or caffeine increases our bodies' levels of endorphins and serotonin naturally occurring chemicals that affect mood.

Attitudes That Empower

There are many attitudes that can empower and enhance results. What we pay attention to determines how we feel. If we pay attention to feeling overwhelmed or stressed, that is how we will feel. Feeling overwhelmed or discouraged can sabotage an entire project. If we pay attention to courage or determination, we can become courageous and determined. Choose the following attitudes that will help you most:

Confident	**Adventurous**	**Focused**
Enthusiastic	**Comfortable**	**Secure**
Inspired	**Peaceful**	**Curious**
Happy	**Relaxed**	**Open-minded**
Joyous	**Courageous**	**Willing to take a risk**

Two primary feelings or emotions—pleasure and pain—motivate us toward or away from results, respectively. These are sometimes called the carrot and the stick. Our desire to increase levels of pleasure and avoid pain in our lives explains much of why we do what we do. When we seek a result, it is not so much the result we're after, but how it will make us *feel* emotionally upon completion.

Write down all of the reasons why you want to achieve your result. The more reasons you have, the more likely it is you will sustain your momentum through the challenge.

Reasons for achieving my result:

_____

_____

Attitudes That Inhibit

Fear is one of the most inhibiting emotions of success. It can prevent the start of the journey or stop us in our tracks. It is said that we are born with two innate fears: the fear of falling and the fear of loud noises. Both of these boil down to fear of the unknown. Fear is not bad in and of itself. It increases adrenaline and functions as a survival mechanism to protect us from danger. With increased adrenaline, you can run faster, think more clearly, or give a more dynamic presentation. We all experience fear at some point and in varying degrees. Successful individuals face their fears, however, and do what needs to be done. Some of the ways to deal with fear include focusing on the importance of the results, making a plan, troubleshooting, having faith in yourself, and taking baby steps.

Challenge Increasing Your Influence

Influence is your ability to focus and direct energy to work with, for, without, and through others to achieve goals. Some people have powerful capabilities to influence individuals, groups of people, things, or an entire course of events. Their influence can sway results based on charisma, prestige, wealth, ability, or position.

There are many situations in which you may want to increase your influence. From the following list, check (✔) those that apply to you:

❏ Reaching agreement on a course of action or job roles

❏ Maintaining a balance between work life and home life

❏ Getting others to complete deadlines or projects

❏ Having others accept your creative ideas

❏ Getting others to follow through on their commitments

❏ Persuading others to accept your opinion

❏ Having your expectations accepted by others

❏ Getting your proposal accepted

❏ Other:

Influence is based on your ability to use emotional, physical, and mental resources to direct outcomes. These resources may include changes in behaviors, the environment, or work that's completed. The core of personal influencing power is energy. How much do you have? How are you directing it?

Some ways to increase influence include persuasion, assertiveness, reasoning, logic, asking questions, being charismatic, and listening.

Challenge
Testing and Monitoring the Plan

Put your plan into action and monitor progress. This means creating a special "dashboard" of gauges and metrics to measure performance along the way. Some calculations could be performed and tracked on a computer, but paper and pencil are also effective. For example, you may need to calculate average sales, revenue per salesperson, or gross margins on your major products or services, and then create a chart or graph to track progress. For a personal goal, you can keep track of your progress in your day planner. Establish milestones and make adjustments in the plan as necessary.

During a visit to one of his steel mills as the day shift was leaving, industrialist Charles Schwab is reported to have written on the floor the number of parts created by the day shift. The night shift saw the number and interpreted it as a challenge to produce more than the day shift. They did, and wrote their number on the floor as well. This continued day after day, with productivity continuing to soar, all because someone wrote a number down for all to see.

How will you monitor your plan?

_____

_____

Challenge Creatively Tinkering

Sometimes you simply will not know what to do until you get into the challenge stage and "play" around with it. Creative tinkering enables you to innovate, experiment, let go of the need to control outcomes, and come up with answers to unanswerable questions. By allowing for adventure and play, you may come up with outcomes more spectacular than you previously imagined.

The creative mind contains the seed for all solutions. It has no gender; it is intuitive and logical. When solving a problem, we're tempted to dwell on it, worry about it, and talk about it. Of course, it's important to define the problem first, but the creative, tinkering mind thinks in terms of possibilities and solutions. The idea is to stimulate the answer, rather than dwell on the problem. First, we need an inquiring, curious mind.

Following are samples of "tinkering" questions. Check (✔) those that will help you get started:

- ❏ What would it be like if I tried this?

- ❏ What if I _____ (fill in the appropriate wording, e.g., changed the color, turned it upside down, and so on)?

- ❏ Is this really necessary?

- ❏ What would it be like if I had what I wanted?

- ❏ How would the ideal make me feel?

- ❏ Who else has solved this?

- ❏ What did they do?

The tinkering mind thinks itself into the realities of what it wants and then invents answers. Creative questions enable the mind to access the solution that already exists. Creative tinkerers such as scientists, inventors, artists, or entrepreneurs ask a question, gather bits of information, listen to their gut, and warehouse it all in the mind. Eventually, they are so saturated with aspects of the answer that it falls into place. Eureka!

Do You Tinker?

Consider how you creatively tinker when solving problems:

➤ Are you playful with problems and solutions, willing to experiment?

➤ Do you take tinkering seriously, but remain relaxed enough to allow the solution to unfold?

➤ Do you allow for the incubation of information?

➤ Do you look at data *and* feelings when problem solving?

➤ Are you energized by the discovery process?

➤ Do you enjoy uncertainty—bringing order to chaos, piecing together puzzles, and solving mysteries?

➤ Do you have a clear vision of where you're going?

Tinkering vs. Tampering

Tinkering is constructive play that leads to improvements. Tampering, on the other hand, unravels the benefits of what has already been accomplished, causing you to lose ground. Here's how you can tell the difference:

Tinkering	Tampering
Simplifies	Complicates
Decreases steps	Increases steps
Measurable	Subjective evaluation
Removes barriers	Creates barriers
Improves morale	Decreases morale
Customer focus mandatory	Customer focus optional

If you decide to tinker, keep a backup of the old version so you can always revert to it if no improvement has been made. If tinkering gives birth to a new and improved version, you can safely move on without burning your bridges behind you.

The irony is that we are all creative individuals, but adults often lose confidence in that power. In fact, people by nature resist change and innovation. In 1899, the director of the U.S. Patent Office said, "Everything that can be invented has been invented," and requested that the Patent Office be dissolved!

Jack Welch, CEO of General Electric, says that to establish a great organization, people need to "have the freedom to be creative, a place that brings out the best in everybody."

We are only limited by the limits of our imagination. Creativity cannot flourish in organizations that have rigid structures or that are top-heavy with inflexible programs. Creative tinkering is inspired by a vision and mindset devoted to continuous improvement, exploration, and innovation. By allowing for creative freedom in the process of achieving, we celebrate the best of the human spirit.

Prize–Reaping the Results

"*Success is getting what you want; happiness is wanting what you've got.*"

–Anonymous

What Are Prizes?

Prizes are the rewards of your journey. They are the results, including feedback, learning experiences, reflections, evaluations, judgments, summaries, appraisals, revelations, settlements, or any other forms of conclusion. In order for prizes to be of value, they need to be examined by the individuals or groups whose lives they affect. In so doing, we learn the truth of the journey.

Truths are the ultimate prizes. They teach us about ourselves, what is of value and purposeful. One truth many discover is that the adventure is its own reward. The adventure may be perilous and the outcome unknown and beyond your control. Embarking on that adventure, however, and the experience it brings, will reward you with increased knowledge and confidence regardless of the tangible results. According to Joseph Campbell, each of us is a completely unique creature: If we are ever to give any gift to the world, it must come from our own experience and the fulfillment of our own potentialities, and not someone else's.

It is essential to stop at the Prize stage and collect the gains from your experience. Without a stopping point, there is never closure to the journey, only perpetual challenge. Think of it as having reached the top of a mountain. When you stop occasionally to look back down the mountain, you appreciate how far you've come.

Prize Stage Tasks

Although you may not gain the result you intended, you might find deeper aspects to the Prize that could be of greater value or benefit than the original goal. To fully gain from your efforts, there are four tasks at the Prize stage:

➤ Evaluating your results

➤ Gaining learning experiences

➤ Reaping rewards and recognition

➤ Gaining inner wealth

The journey is never complete at the Prize stage, however. Once you have reached your results, you must return Home and begin the process again. Having learned from your previous experiences, the next revolution around the cycle will allow you to ask better questions, create a more effective plan of action, and reap more worthwhile payoffs. In this way, you ensure continuous growth and learning—a hallmark of quality and excellence.

Evaluating Your Results

This is the point at which you examine your result against your vision, mission, goals, and standards. Did you achieve what you had planned? Was it worth the time and effort? Part of your examination needs to address the quality of your result.

Quality control is a way of determining if you've achieved the results you set out to accomplish. It reveals the essential truth of the matter. It's what counts, but it does not come easily. Quality depends on the right people, tools, strategy, and circumstances all coming together. The following questions will help you assess the quality of your results. Check (✔) those that describe your result:

❏ Quality conformance: Does your result conform to the standards and expectations established at Home?

❏ Does your result satisfy the criteria for worthwhile results (strategic, balanced, selfless, and enduring)?

❏ Effectiveness: Does the result "work"? Does the result do what you wanted it to do? If it's a product, does it perform its task "as advertised"?

❏ Reliability: Is the result something that can be depended upon for a specified length of time?

❏ Quantity: Did you achieve the amount you set out to achieve?

❏ Satisfaction: Are you happy with the result? If not, what can you do differently to change the situation?

❏ Other:

What about imperfect results? Because quality is a moving target defined by those setting the standards, in a sense nothing is ever perfect, and we are never truly finished. We are constantly in a state of improvement, and there's always more to be done. In business, the race belongs to the swift. One of the reasons why Bill Gates, founder of Microsoft, won his race for software dominance can be summed up as follows: *Finished is better than perfect.*

Gaining Learning Experiences

All experiences teach lessons. Learning experiences are based on our ability to stop, look, listen, and learn. Learning experiences are what transform us from what we were to a new, evolved version of ourselves.

If we represent the life experience as a fruit tree, some people are content to sit on the inner branches and stare out at the fruit that hangs on the limbs. They remain unchanged, untested, and unfulfilled in the bounty that life offers. Others boldly climb out on the limbs, pick the fruit, and savor its sweet rewards. The fruit is the prize of the journey. Sometimes the fruit is a learning experience. If the fruit is bitter, you learn to focus your efforts elsewhere. If the goal is difficult to reach, but worth the effort, you find better ways to reach it.

The following questions can help you maximize your learning experiences:

➤ What result was achieved?

➤ What went right in each of the stages?

➤ What went wrong in each of the stages?

➤ What would you do differently next time?

➤ What have you learned about yourself?

➤ What have you learned about others?

➤ What hidden truths have become apparent?

➤ What was your most important lesson?

Unfortunately, not all efforts bring about successful changes. These are the failed attempts, mistakes, setbacks, and missed opportunities, but within every failure is a learning experience.

Technically, achieving results means you've achieved your goal. Goals are the measure of success. Does this mean you have failed if you have not achieved your goals? No, not if you're paying attention and continuously learning. Many corporate giants have learned from their failures, turning them into future successes and achieving lofty goals. Let's look at this idea of "failure."

Failure Through Effort

When people make an effort to take risks and implement change, mistakes happen. You cannot win unless you play the game. Thomas Watson, founder of IBM, said that if you want to be successful, "increase your failure rate." In fact, generally the bigger the risk, the bigger the payoff. This is not gambling, however. You must calculate the odds at the outset, make every attempt to minimize risk, and pave a successful route; but in the end, be prepared to face disappointment. If the effort was in alignment with the mission and core values, and in the interests of the organization, customers, and shareholders, the failure is forgivable. The effort itself should be rewarded to reinforce that it is safe to take risks and learn from mistakes.

Describe a result that "failed" through your efforts:

_____

_____

Failure Through Laziness

We all have an energetic side and a lazy side. You may work 60 hours a week and fulfill personal responsibilities with vigor, but laziness shows up disguised as fear. Fear is the force that prevents us from changing the status quo. Anything new—such as information, procedures, or relationships—can be very threatening. It means leaving behind what's familiar and making room for the unfamiliar, and that takes work. For some, the work of assimilation can be so terrifying that it's easier to just stay put. Remember, however, that we have numerous resources available to bring about positive change. Change is reinventing how we work and live, from relating and politicking to consuming, communicating, and even procreating. Change is inevitable and offers tremendous potential for the human race. Much like a stream, if you're not doing the work of "flowing" with change, you're stagnant.

Describe a situation in which you "failed" through laziness (fear of change):

_____

_____

By shifting our thinking, we can rewrite the rules so that there is no failure. Post-it® notes emerged from a failed attempt to invent a new adhesive glue. Scotchguard™ was born when a researcher noticed that chemicals spilled onto sneakers kept them clean. Apple computer made quantum advances when Xerox refused to take on the "mouse." Xerox was born when IBM rebuffed their technology as impractical.

Following are some important lessons of experience:

➤ **Timing can be critical.** Sometimes you have the right goal, the right people, the right skills, and the right resources, but the timing is wrong.

➤ **Learn from your mistakes.** Learning from mistakes is based on our ability to let go and move on.

➤ **People have hidden talents.** The change process demands that we develop parts of ourselves that lie dormant until called upon.

➤ **We want the new, but hang on to the past.** In spite of our efforts to forge something new, we cling to what we know. To learn, we must allow opportunities for new things to happen.

➤ **Recognize when enough is enough.** Declare yourself a winner by knowing when to cut losses, change direction, or end the project.

➤ **Money is not the true reward.** Money is a reward, but most people are ultimately seeking something other than monetary gain.

➤ **Be aware of serendipity.** Serendipity is the gift of finding valuable things not sought after. Within every problem is a gift, sometimes hidden.

Reaping Rewards and Recognition

Prize

Rewards and recognition are another form of positive payoffs from results. They act as powerful reinforcement, encouraging us to repeat whatever behavior led to the reward.

Compensation is what you give people for doing the work they were asked or hired to do. Rewards and recognition, on the other hand, celebrate successes and effort beyond the call of duty. Rewarding a person's attempts for success is also a powerful reinforcement.

Recognition for a job well done is the top motivator of performance.

If you want people to align themselves with missions, they must be rewarded or recognized for successful completion of goals that support the mission. If reward systems are not properly implemented, however, they can negatively affect performance. Morale decreases instead of increases. For example, if rewards are not consistent, are of no value to the recipient, are out of proportion to the achievement, or are rarely given, they can create resentment and distrust of the system.

Guidelines for Providing Rewards and Recognition

➤ Give rewards that individuals value

To encourage appropriate behaviors, know what is of value to each individual. Awarding tickets to a football game in recognition of winning a sales contest won't be motivation for an employee bored by sports. Tailor rewards by finding out what each person values.

➤ Give rewards proportionate to the performance

Rewards should be in balance with the achievement. Give informal recognition for daily or expected results. Give formal recognition for more exceptional results. Rules of thumb: For every four informal rewards (thank-you note, verbal compliment, and so on), give one formal acknowledgment. For every four formal acknowledgments, give one high-prestige reward (plaque, ceremony, and so on).

➤ Give rewards in a timely manner

The sooner the reward is provided after the desired behavior, the more likely the behavior will be repeated. Tell the recipient why you are rewarding him or her. Consistently reward the performance whenever it occurs; as the behavior becomes a habit or routine, more occasional recognition is acceptable.

➤ If no one gives you a reward for achieving positive results, reward yourself

There is joy in accomplishing missions and goals. If no one formally presents you with a reward, give yourself a personalized pat on the back. Treat yourself to something special to celebrate your results.

No-Cost Reward and Recognition Ideas

Open praise. Tell people that you appreciate their help and that they did a great job.

Great Job Awards. Print "Great Job Award" on desktop tent cards. Anyone can use them when someone does a great job.

Personal email or note of thanks. Email or write a quick thank-you note.

Signatures on company literature. Document the team's results in an announcement or brochure for company distribution. Have everyone involved sign the document. This increases active participation in projects by others and indicates pride and ownership from the team.

Congratulations board. Publicly post good news and congratulatory remarks. Make sure everyone gets on the board. Help others to earn the right.

Bravo cards. Write "Bravo!" on a tent card, with your reinforcing statement on the inside. Give it to the person you are recognizing along with your verbal praise.

Bell ringing. Ring a handheld bell when an individual's goal or quota has been reached.

Group sharing. Have everyone at a meeting share success stories and positive comments.

Post-it® notes. Use Post-it® notes with positive pre-printed messages and add your personal thanks. Post them prominently on the wall of those you wish to thank.

Others:

➤ Letter from manager or president/owner

➤ Personal phone call from president/owner

➤ Special parking space

➤ Answer the recipient's phone for a day

➤ Wash the person's car

➤ Banner in the lunchroom

88

Low-Cost Reward and Recognition Ideas

➤ Time off (days off, a half-day off, or Friday off)

➤ Flowers and/or balloons

➤ Movie tickets

➤ Dinner for two at a favorite restaurant

➤ Book of their choice

➤ Day planner

➤ Internet connection

➤ Lunch

➤ New briefcase/suitcase

➤ Gardener or cook for a day

➤ Seminar or class of the recipient's choice

➤ Club membership or day at a spa

➤ Bagels for a year, one per week

➤ A toy or novelty that relates to the accomplishment

Ideas for Formal Rewards and Prizes

Use the following examples to acknowledge significant achievements that span a longer time, such as major campaigns and incentive plans. The significance placed on the award is what counts.

trip/vacation	special bulletin	cook for a week
car	stereo	shopping spree
trophy	television	office furniture
jewelry	watch	mobile phone
house cleaning	gold pen	computer
spa/salon package	artwork	champagne

Prize Gaining Inner Wealth

Inner wealth is the positive emotional payoff we achieve from results. It's the sum total of good feelings we experience *internally* because of our external achievements. Inner wealth adds meaning, joy, or purposefulness to the journey, providing the sensation of "arrival." People seek and achieve because they ultimately want to feel good about themselves and what they do.

Here are some examples of how achieving results leads to the deeper rewards of inner wealth:

Result	Inner Wealth
buying a house	pride
winning an election	elation
meaningful career	sense of purpose, contribution
supportive family	connection and legacy
balancing a budget	relief
streamlining a department	appreciation
hiring a talented employee	comfort
company funding	security
flying to the moon	adventure
Other: _____	Other: _____
_____	_____

Inner Wealth Deposits

When a problem is solved, a relationship is mended, or a project is finished, a sense of completion creates relief. The tension created from the gap between where you were and where you wanted to be has been resolved, and that resolution gives rise to a wide range of inner wealth fulfillment.

Imagine that your financial wealth is stored in a bank. That wealth grows with interest and by making additional deposits. We build our inner wealth by adding to our inner "bank balance." If what we do produces favorable results, it adds to fulfillment. The more Prizes, the bigger the inner bank balance. The larger the internal wealth, the more strength we gain for facing the next challenge.

Setbacks, disappointments, or failed attempts cause emotional withdrawals from the account. If we have a sufficient balance after a withdrawal, however, there is enough capacity on reserve to rebound and keep going. If the balance is too low, however, one devastating event could overdraw the account. Emotional bankruptcy leads to depression, despair, and hopelessness. We have a right to grieve over losses, but it is important to restore our ability to "make deposits." Maintaining strong inner wealth—gained through wins both large and small—helps people get through the tough times, promotes emotional healing, and improves the quality of life.

Inner wealth deposits come in many forms. From the following list, check (✔) those that you will be able deposit upon achieving your desired result:

❑ Joy	❑ Security	❑ Contribution	❑ Powerful
❑ Happy	❑ Free	❑ Insightful	❑ Complete
❑ Fulfilled	❑ Adventurous	❑ Grateful	❑ Dignified
❑ Satisfied	❑ Relieved	❑ Generous	❑ Loving
❑ Authentic	❑ Delighted	❑ Compassionate	❑ Illuminated
❑ Peaceful	❑ Creative	❑ Connected	❑ Comfortable
❑ Accomplished	❑ Proud	❑ Exhilarated	❑ Empathic
❑ Assured	❑ Forgiving	❑ Respectful	❑ Centered
❑ Confident	❑ Competent	❑ Appreciation	❑ Benevolent
❑ Calm	❑ Soothed	❑ Loved	❑ Harmonious

INNER WEALTH PAYOFFS

Think back over your five biggest accomplishments. What were your inner wealth payoffs?

1. _____

2. _____

3. _____

4. _____

5. _____

When are you most joyful?

When are you at your best?

Are there any common denominators to these experiences? If so, what are they?

When and how often do they occur?

When you felt sorrowful, despairing, or lost, what brought you back to life?

How is what you're currently doing preventing you from increasing your inner wealth?

How can you increase your inner wealth bank balance?

Going Home and Beginning Again

Even if you're on the right track, if you sit there too long, you'll get run over."

—Will Rogers

Once you've collected Prizes, go Home and begin the process again. No matter the outcome of your journey, going Home helps you continue the change process with renewed opportunities for improvement. At Home, ask better questions, rethink the mission if necessary, set new goals, and revise standards and expectations if necessary. Go on to Help, gather resources, learn skills, and create a better plan. Test the plan in the Challenge stage, and then collect Prizes. And so the cycle goes.

The temptation to bask in the joy of the Prize is strong. Reaching goals feels good, but it can also lure us into thinking that we're "done." Personal and organizational greatness is achieved only by continuing the process. The key is not to lock in on the successes, but to continue to set ever-higher goals and standards.

Never let successes or other results cause you to "plateau." Every person reaches a plateau in his or her progress at some point—the diet doesn't seem to be working, the project seems stale, the challenge becomes boring. Every growing organization, no matter how dramatic its growth, reaches a leveling effect, be it with products, services, or relationships. These are times to regroup and rethink your strategy, establish new goals and the actions needed to achieve them.

The return Home is not only required to complete the process, but also to begin the process again while you are still strong. In this way, success creates momentum for growth. All people and organizations reach a point of maturity and begin to slow down, a process sometimes depicted as an "S" curve. If things get easier, you'll know you've reached a plateau.

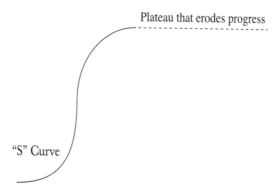

You can avoid the effects of stagnation and erosion by jumping the "S" curve. Keep progressing after each victory. You can take advantage of the momentum you've gained and make additional improvements from a position of strength.

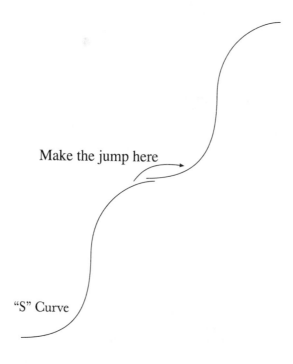

The Spiral of Renewal

The nature of change dictates that you can never truly go back to the same place. You can't actually go Home again because you have evolved, one way or another. There may still be the "look" of the old—there will still be telephone calls to make and papers to file and traffic to sit in, but you will be different. As you incorporate your new wisdom and tap into your deeper sense of identity, Home becomes the starting point of continuous renewal.

Returning Home enables us to see the effects of the results achieved. If you choose to continue to evolve, the journey does not fold back in on itself as a circular cycle (see Figure A), but forms a spiral (see Figure B). Spirals occur in nature as evidence of the evolutionary path of growth or change, but they also have an inhibiting factor that keeps growth from spinning out of control. The new journey begins at a higher level than before. This time you're wiser and more prepared for the road ahead.

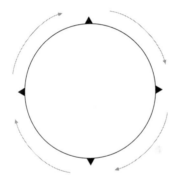

Figure A: No growth or learning—perpetual wheel spinning

Figure B: Evolutionary, controlled growth

Putting the Process to Work

> *The secret of getting ahead is getting started. The secret of getting started is breaking your complex overwhelming tasks into small manageable tasks, and then starting on the first one."*
>
> –Mark Twain

How Personality Styles Affect Results

Circumstances do not always work in ways that support our goals. For example, not everyone will follow the logical sequence of stages in the journey, nor will others support or enlist in your cause.

Personality types also affect how people participate in the journey. Four personality or behavioral styles have been identified as far back as the father of medicine, Hippocrates; and later, psychologist Carl Jung. While each of us exhibits traits of all four types, one type tends to define our style, feels more comfortable than the others, and influences how we get things done. It is called a "preferred" personality style. Find your own style among the following, which describe how each preferred style *tends* to interact with the achievement process.

Accommodators, Relators, or Amiables. Some people do not leave Home willingly. They are content to keep the home fires burning, and need encouragement to change or leave security against their will. This personality type values working for other people; needs reassurances, strong guidance, and clear expectations; and takes smaller steps in getting started.

Thinkers, or Analyzers. Others leave Home, head for Help, but return Home again—going to another seminar, having another meeting, reading another book, thinking and gathering more information, hesitant to move on. This task-oriented style mostly enjoys working alone, gathering information and analyzing, and needs clear guidelines and deadlines to keep on track.

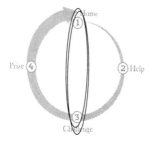

Controllers, Directors, or Drivers. This personality type thinks they don't need Help, bypasses the Help stage completely, and heads straight for the Challenge without assistance from anyone or anything. Controllers like working *through* other people; they are focused on results but they need to develop flexibility in working with others, allowing for discovery along the way.

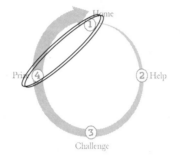

Influencers, or Socializers. Finally, there are those that think, "Prizes? That's for me!" Influencers head straight for the payoffs in the form of daydreams and promises, without putting in the effort. These personality types work well with other people, make great team players, are creative risk takers, and need to develop focus and stay organized throughout the process. It's easy for this type to be distracted by side issues.

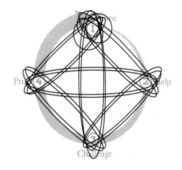

Chaos. What happens when each personality style goes for results without a clear vision of the process? Chaos. Instead of going around in circles and not getting anywhere, undisciplined approaches figuratively go around in ovals.

An organized approach. When the process is followed in a logical sequence, you increase efficiency and effectiveness in producing desirable outcomes. Unfortunately, circumstances do not always neatly line up in a sequence. You may be unwillingly thrown out of Home into the Challenge with no time for Help, or be tempted to go back to the Help stage to rethink your plan. It's important however, to keep moving forward *through* the process. You cannot learn how to improve the plan until you reach the Prize stage where real learning takes place.

Understanding the Styles

Locate your preferred personality style in the following charts, remembering that we are all motivated by various aspects of each style at different times. Use the guidelines in the second column for ideas to get you "unstuck."

Accommodators	
Motivations	**How to Get Unstuck**
Recognition for service	Be more open to change
Sincerity; genuine appreciation	Reward yourself for good work
Security in all situations	Feel good about accomplishments
More time to adjust to change	Get introduced to new groups
Limited territory	Create goals that support mission
Identification with others	Put fear aside and "just do it"
Simple, repeated procedures	Use more strategic approaches

Thinkers	
Motivations	**How to Get Unstuck**
Known operating procedures	Be mindful of deadlines
No sudden or abrupt change	Listen to your "gut" (intuition), not just your head
Controlled environment	More self-confidence
Reassurance	Larger perspective beyond your own
Working alone	Courage to speak up in group settings
Personal attention to objectives	Tolerance of ambiguity
References; verification of facts	Appreciation of other's explanations

Controllers	
Motivations	**How to Get Unstuck**
Power and authority, often financial	Accept help; there's more to learn
New and varied activities	Working in groups or teams
Direct answers and efficient operations	Accept merits of intangible rewards
Knowing "bottom-line" payoffs	Use pacing and relaxation
Challenges and no controls	Be a better listener
Knowing the "big picture" of the operation	Show empathy, patience, and tolerance
Prestige; position; advancement	Be aware that rules exist for a reason

Influencers	
Motivations	**How to Get Unstuck**
Popularity; social recognition	Do the steps, don't just talk about them
People to talk to; teamwork	Manage time more effectively
Group activities outside of the job	Think about consequences of actions
Casual, warm relationships	Be more organized; mindful of deadlines
Freedom from control	Break tasks down into units
Approval and friendliness	Slow down to analyze data
Public recognition with awards	Develop emotional control

How do we deal with the chaos of different personality types working in ovals? Chaos is not necessarily bad. In fact, there may be a strange symmetry in the disorder. When plans don't work, the temptation is to back up–to pick up over-looked information or resources, or to rethink the plan. The irony is that some-times you have to step backward in order to move forward. Ultimately, what's important is to *keep moving.* If things aren't working, go to the Prize stage, where learning takes place. Learn through feedback, reflection, and evaluation. Go Home and begin the process again by asking better questions. What went wrong? What do I need to change? What's my new plan? Only in this way will you evolve to the next higher level of growth toward results without spinning your wheels.

Evolutionary, controlled growth

All movement will eventually move you forward. Focus on results, never get stuck in one stage too long, and learn to feel comfortable in each stage. Learn to feel at "Home" in every stage and you will learn to enjoy the process. The ideal road map or game plan is a spiral cycle, creating an organized, efficient approach that continuously allows for growth and revitalization. The spiral is the only approach that enhances success by streamlining time, effort, and energy. It re-flects an evolutionary process that gets you where you want to go.

Achieving Desired Results: Examples

Following are two examples of desired results—one for a personal goal, the other for a professional goal. Both examples include complete details about what the process might look like for each stage and task. These are best-case scenarios. If you were using either of these plans and it failed, you could easily diagnose the weak link in the process and make revisions in that area. Keep in mind, however, that a change in one area may have a domino effect, causing changes, positive or negative, in other areas. As in a game of chess, consider how your actions affect the entire plan.

Personal Example: Losing Weight

HOME

Questions:	What do I want?
Mission:	Lose weight *so that* I feel and look my best.
Goal:	Lose 25 pounds in six months. Establish starting weight as a baseline measurement.
Standards:	Lose weight without compromising health; improve muscle strength.

HELP

Resources:	Buy book on dieting. Consult with nutritionist and doctor. Buy supplements and exercise video.
Empower:	Take personal responsibility for making changes without excuses.
Skills:	Learn about balanced diets, effective food combinations, and appropriate supplements.
Action Plan:	Create a start date and plan for meals, supplements, and exercise.

CHALLENGE

Attitude:	Focus on a long-term, lifestyle change. Give myself daily encouragement.
Influence:	Control influence by controlling circumstances; cut back on restaurant eating; eat to taste.
Test/Monitor Plan:	Implement plan; monitor weight-loss progress on scale weekly.
Creatively Tinker:	Experiement with the plan as necessary if I plateau.

PRIZE

Evaluate Results:	Measure result at end of six months; check energy levels and pounds.
Rewards/Recognition:	Reward myself with a treat (new wardrobe? spa day? vacation?).
Learning Experiences:	Learned what worked, how I overcame obstacles, and how to stay on track.
Inner Wealth:	Increased self-esteem, pride, confidence, energy, increased opportunities, more fun.

Organizational Example: Empowering Employees

HOME

Questions:	What do I want?
Mission:	Increase employee empowerment to unleash creative problem solving (*so that* is implied in *to*)
Goal:	Implement 10 new innovative product lines within one year
Standards:	Products must conform to quality standards, have zero defects, and meet consumer safety standards; set weekly meeting expectations and boundaries of authority; write job descriptions and standards of excellence

HELP

Resources:	500K budget; training room; trainers; rewards
Empower:	Decisions, planning, informing, developing, monitoring, rewarding, and feedback
Skills:	Teach employees about empowerment, how to solve problems, be creative, and assert ideas
Action Plan:	Set training schedule; product idea contest; implement reward system; weekly meetings; identify obstacles to performance and remove obstacles beyond the control of employees

CHALLENGE

Attitude:	Inspire through encouragement; on-the-spot praise; coaching; mentoring program
Influence:	Weekly one-on-ones with employees to guide progress
Test/Monitor:	Implement plan and track progress
Creatively Tinker:	Allow for creative play, discovery, and mistakes

PRIZE

Evaluate Results:	Evaluate results against standards and goals
Rewards/Recognition:	Give recognition; reward discoveries and effort, regardless of outcome
Learning Experiences:	Share lessons with all; give feedback; look for serendipity; learn from mistakes
Inner Wealth:	Gain satisfaction from the journey; begin again

Good vs. Great Organizational Results

When seeking organizational results, you can strive for good results or great results. Good organizations work to maintain the status quo. Great organizations are continually dissatisfied, meaning they do not stop at the Prize stage. They begin the process repeatedly, each time improving their results. By making the right choices in each stage, you too can achieve organizational greatness.

Compare the good and great organizations in the following chart, which shows how small differences at each stage add up to big differences in the end. Great organizations create a more fulfilled, exciting workplace for employees, while consistently reaping the rewards of increased profits, competitive advantage, and customer loyalty. Check (✔) those tendencies that best describe your organization.

Good vs. Great

Good Organizations (Complacent)	Great Organizations (Continually Dissatisfied)
HOME	
Questions: periodically question status quo to make improvements	**Questions:** continually question status quo to make improvements
Mission: set generic missions to meet explicit needs of customers; seek to meet and keep boundaries	**Mission:** set grand missions to meet explicit and implicit wants and needs of customers, constantly create more room for growth
Goals: periodically set goals that stretch past records	**Goals:** continually push the limits of the envelope
Standards: analyze and improve substandard departments; employees find importance in what they do to maintain high performance levels and protect their position	**Standards:** analyze and improve best-performing departments; employees analyze the process of what created their successes and use this to raise the bar even further
HELP	
Resources: mostly promote from within to build morale and loyalty	**Resources:** balance hiring from within and from external sources to bring in fresh ideas
Empower: assign the implementation of an idea to individuals other than the creator; aggressively solve problems	**Empower:** encourage generators of ideas to take their own initiative; aggressively look for new opportunities
Skills: stick with core competencies of each individual; employees seek to fit in with the group	**Skills:** examine unassociated connections for new synergistic alliances; develop skills to determine how to be different
Plan: create template strategic action plans that provide a roadmap to the future, and adjust as needed to stay on course	**Plan:** use strategic action plans as a loose framework, which is continually fine-tuned

Good Organizations (Complacent)	Great Organizations (Continually Dissatisfied)
CHALLENGE	
Attitude: employees confident in abilities: "if it's not broke, don't fix it."	**Attitude:** employees continually test themselves: "If it's easy, it's not worth doing because everyone else can do it too."
Influence: play by the rules	**Influence:** change the game and make new rules
Test: minimize risk for maximum benefit	**Test:** enter the test aggressively with prudent risk
Creative Tinkering: believe the system is important; conform to structure	**Creative Tinkering:** believe that individuals are important; seek originality; constantly seek to create ideas and ways to implement them
PRIZE	
Results: have no consistent measure for results	**Results:** fanatically measure results that matter
Rewards: work to develop all low-performing employees; offer inconsistent rewards	**Rewards:** abundantly and consistently reward the most productive, creative employees
Learning: learn from mistakes	**Learning:** seek continuous learning; share lessons with other employees or team members
Inner Wealth: employees are satisfied when they've reached goals	**Inner Wealth:** employees find joy in the entire process of achieving

Worksheet

Your Desired Result: _____

HOME
Questions: What do you want? _____

_____

Mission: _____

_____

Goal: _____

_____

Standards: _____

_____

HELP
Resources: _____

_____

Empower: _____

_____

Skills: _____

_____

Action Plan: _____

_____

CHALLENGE

Attitude: _____

_____

Influence: _____

_____

Test and Monitor the Plan: _____

_____

Creatively Tinker: _____

_____

PRIZE

Evaluate Results: _____

_____

Rewards and Recognition: _____

_____

Learning Experiences: _____

_____

Inner Wealth: _____

_____

Additional Reading

Bardwick, Judith. *Danger in the Comfort Zone*. New York: AMACOM, 1991.

Buckingham, Marcus and Curt Coffman. *First, Break All the Rules*. New York: Simon & Schuster Inc., 1999.

Campbell, Joseph. *The Power of Myth*. New York: Doubleday, 1988.

Faust, Gerald W., Richard I. Lyles, and Will Phillips. *Responsible Managers Get Results*. New York: AMACOM, 1998.

Gerzon, Robert. *Finding Serenity in the Age of Anxiety*. London: Macmillan, 1997.

Kaplan, Robert and David Norton. *The Strategy-Focused Organization*. Boston: Harvard Business School Press, 2001.

Kouzes, James and Barry Posner. *The Leadership Challenge*. San Francisco: Jossey-Bass Publishers, 1987.

Riso, Don Richard. *Personality Types*. Boston, MA: Houghton Mifflin Company, 1996.

Senge, Peter. *The Fifth Discipline*. New York: Doubleday Currency, 1990.

Smallwood, Norm, Dave Ulrich, and Jack Zenger. *Results-Based Leadership*. Boston: Harvard Business School Press, 1999.